# NEW DIRECTIONS FOR ADULT AND CONTINUING EDUCATION

Ralph G. Brockett, *University of Tennessee, Knoxville*
EDITOR-IN-CHIEF

Alan B. Knox, *University of Wisconsin, Madison*
CONSULTING EDITOR

# Creating Environments for Effective Adult Learning

Roger Hiemstra
*Syracuse University*

*EDITOR*

Number 50, Summer 1991

JOSSEY-BASS INC., PUBLISHERS, San Francisco

MAXWELL MACMILLAN INTERNATIONAL PUBLISHING GROUP
New York • Oxford • Singapore • Sydney • Toronto

CREATING ENVIRONMENTS FOR EFFECTIVE ADULT LEARNING
*Roger Hiemstra* (ed.)
New Directions for Adult and Continuing Education, no. 50
*Ralph G. Brockett,* Editor-in-Chief
*Alan B. Knox,* Consulting Editor

Microfilm copies of issues and articles are available in 16mm and 35mm, as well as microfiche in 105mm, through University Microfilms Inc., 300 North Zeeb Road, Ann Arbor, Michigan 48106.

LC 85-644750          ISSN 0195-2242          ISBN 1-55542-784-7

NEW DIRECTIONS FOR ADULT AND CONTINUING EDUCATION is part of The Jossey-Bass Higher and Adult Education Series and is published quarterly by Jossey-Bass Inc., Publishers, 350 Sansome Street, San Francisco, California 94104-1310 (publication number USPS 493-930). Second-class postage paid at San Francisco, California, and at additional mailing offices. POSTMASTER: Send address changes to New Directions for Adult and Continuing Education, Jossey-Bass Inc., Publishers, 350 Sansome Street, San Francisco, California 94104-1310.

SUBSCRIPTIONS for 1991 cost $45.00 for individuals and $60.00 for institutions, agencies, and libraries.

EDITORIAL CORRESPONDENCE should be sent to the Editor-in-Chief, Ralph G. Brockett, Dept. of Technological and Adult Education, University of Tennessee, 402 Claxton Addition, Knoxville, Tennessee 37996-3400.

Cover photograph by Wernher Krutein/PHOTOVAULT © 1990.

Printed on acid-free paper in the United States of America.

# CONTENTS

# EDITOR'S NOTES

The word "environment" often is associated either with a physical setting or, more recently, with the multiple ecosystems in which we live. When "learning" is asociated with "environment," various meanings are conjured up in the minds of adult educators, such as the learning climate, the physical environment, the psychological or emotional climate, and the social setting. This volume, *Environments for Effective Adult Learning*, presents various ways of thinking about the learning environment in order to enhance the effectiveness of adult teaching and learning processes.

In the following chapters, ten professionals in adult and continuing education present their views about various aspects of effective learning environments. Conceptual analyses, personal experiences in these environments, and reviews of relevant literature are provided. Some of the authors challenge long-held views and practices in ways that may cause discomfort to adherents of conventional wisdom. However, this dissent is offered in the spirit of helping all adult educators change and grow in their efforts to become more effective practitioners. Whenever possible, the authors provide exhibits with checklists that the adult educator can use to examine or guide personal practice.

An appropriate criticism of some of the practical aspects of this volume might be their "positivist" nature. The inclusion of practical experience, models, and checklists is not intended to establish monological certainty of their value. It is my hope that these materials and chapters are not read once and then shelved and forgotten. I want readers to be involved with the information presented and to examine, criticize, and reconstruct it through critical reflections.

In Chapter One, I explore the various meanings of learning environments, describe some associated literature, and provide an organizing framework for the chapters included in this volume. I introduce three broad categories for thinking about learning environments: physical aspects, psychological-emotional aspects, and sociocultural aspects.

In the first of two consecutive chapters related primarily to physical settings, Rodney D. Fulton, in Chapter Two, initiates the difficult process of building a conceptual model for understanding relationships between various components of the physical environment and learner attributes: satisfaction, participation, achievement, transcendent/immanent attributes, authority, and layout (SPATIAL). He challenges readers to examine the SPATIAL model and add to the list of associated questions that he has developed.

Richard S. Vosko, a designer and independent consultant for worship environments, is concerned in Chapter Three that the way physical environments are arranged or manipulated can affect learning experiences.

Referring to himself as a space specialist, he argues that adult educators must become aware of how people use space and urges educators to conduct space "audits."

In an effort to bridge physical settings and learners' personal needs, Judith K. DeJoy, in Chapter Four, describes how microcomputer technology can be incorporated into adult learning environments. She urges adult educators to consider learners' emotions, perceptions, and self-concepts when thinking about instructional design and delivery issues associated with the use of microcomputers. She lists numerous questions to guide adult educators in such thinking.

In Chapter Five, Burton R. Sisco discusses the importance of the first encounter between adult learners and their instructors in terms of establishing positive emotional, psychological, and social settings for subsequent learning. He describes various ways of building an effective climate for learning, including creating trust, developing a positive learning environment, and promoting mutually supportive relationships among learners. He, too, provides a checklist of questions to guide instructors in thinking about the first few hours spent with adult learners.

V. L. Mike Mahoney, in Chapter Six, is concerned about the personal history that each individual brings to the learning setting. Family, job, community, and health problems can create emotional or psychological barriers to learning. He presents four vignettes about real learners with real "baggage" that impeded their learning. Using the metaphor of temperature changes on a thermometer, he creates a device for measuring the relative impact on a person of various life events and suggests what a teacher can do to help learners make appropriate adjustments to overcome impediments to learning.

Chapters Seven and Eight focus on two important social and cultural issues with which many adult educators need to grapple: the impact of race and of gender on the learning environment. In some ways, the placement of these two chapters within the topical area of sociocultural aspects of the learning environmnent is too confining. A person's views of race and gender usually are subjective in nature, existing in the eyes of the beholder, and therefore could be considered psychological or even philosophical in nature. However, my intent in including these two chapters is to facilitate critical thinking about two troublesome social and cultural issues that have not been resolved in the United States or elsewhere.

Scipio A. J. Colin III and Trudie Kibbe Preciphs open Chapter Seven with a quote by William E. B. Dubois who accurately forecasted, almost ninety years ago, that the problem of the color-line would be the problem of this century. Colin and Preciphs suggest that adult educators do not overtly confront racism but instead focus on safe or nonthreatening issues such as low socioeconomic status, motivation, and participation. Their chapter is written to challenge readers, especially white adult educators, to dig deep inside themselves for self-reflection and commitment to positive social change.

Chapter Eight on women, gender, and the learning environment, by Susan Collard and Joyce Stalker, is equally as challenging to the "safer" stances taken on a day-to-day basis by many adult educators. The authors assert that various social and cultural understandings associated with gender differences are related to oppression and exploitation. They describe how the adult education field has historically been dominated by males, a situation that has disempowered women in various ways. They urge educators to make a new commitment to women learners.

In Chapter Nine, Rodney D. Fulton and I provide an annotation of various books, book chapters, monographs, and journal articles related either in general to aspects of the learning environment or to specific ideas presented in the other chapters of this volume. In the final chapter, I summarize and synthesize various themes from the previous chapters. I also provide some suggestions on the kinds of research needed to continue the development of information about effective learning environments.

Roger Hiemstra
Editor

*Roger Hiemstra is professor of adult education and chair of the adult education graduate program at Syracuse University, Syracuse, New York. He is a member of two professional journal editorial boards, the author of numerous publications, and a co-author of two recent books:* Individualizing Instruction: Making Learning Personal, Empowering, and Successful *(1990, with Burton R. Sisco) and* Self-Direction in Adult Learning: Perspectives on Theory, Research, and Practice *(1991, with Ralph G. Brockett).*

*This chapter describes a personal journey to a working definition of learning environments and suggests how ingrained views of these environments can be changed when they impede the learning process.*

# Aspects of Effective Learning Environments

*Roger Hiemstra*

My interest in learning environments is more than two decades old. When I began my university teaching career at the University of Nebraska in 1970, I was basically unprepared for the task. Using as my frame of reference the mainly didactic teaching approaches modeled for me in my formal education, I did lots of lecturing to and testing of learners who I "arranged" in straight rows of chairs facing me. It would actually be more accurate to say that the institution "arranged" the physical setting for me, as many of the rooms in which I taught had unmovable chairs in rows or the "tradition" against rearranging rooms was very strong due to time constraints, learner expectations, and expectations of colleagues who also used the spaces. I survived that first year but did not feel very successful as a teacher. This judgment was confirmed by the evaluation forms completed by the students in my classes.

Fortunately for me and for subsequent learners with whom I have worked, I took my summative course evaluation efforts quite seriously. Through paper-and-pencil devices, personal observations of student interactions, and interviews with learners, I began the process of improving the style and quality of my teaching. My prior work with a more informal educational organization, Cooperative Extension, had given me insights into working with adults that I began to incorporate. I started seeking out various sources on learning climate (Hunsaker and Pierce, 1959; Knowles, 1970), architecture and design (Becker, 1960; Commission on Architecture, 1956), human engineering (Damon, Stoudt, and McFarland, 1966; Woodson and Conover, 1966), audiovisual use and selection (Kemp, 1968), and how people use space (Sommer, 1969). I also began observing how people interacted with learning spaces and I experimented with different room arrangements.

Eventually, this process of self-improvement led to requests from organizations to evaluate their adult learning centers and classrooms and to make recommendations for improvements. I visited their places, talked with participants and instructors, took photographs, measured chairs, tables, and rooms, examined support equipment, and designed some plans for change (Hiemstra, 1976). A career move in 1976 slowed my growth in understanding the physical learning environment, although I continued related experimentation in the classroom.

Another career change in 1980 put me in contact with three colleagues who helped to renew my interest in and involvement with the learning environment. These relationships eventually led to collaborative scholarship. Richard Vosko and I (Vosko and Hiemstra, 1988) together investigated physical features of the learning environment, based on his dissertation research (Vosko, 1984). Burton R. Sisco and I collaborated on a book about the task of teaching adults, which includes material on the learning climate and physical environment (Hiemstra and Sisco, 1990). Ralph Brockett and I collaborated on a book about self-direction in learning, which includes discussion on the learning environment (Brockett and Hiemstra, 1991).

Until about two years ago, my journey had been down a path primarily focused on the physical environment. Then, in the course of approximately six months, I happened to read Belenky, Clinchy, Goldberger, and Tarule (1986), Gilligan (1982), and early drafts of two colleagues' work on gender-related issues in adult education (Hayes, 1989; Hugo, 1990). This was all about the same time Sisco and I were finishing our co-authored book, and the result for me was a sudden awareness that I must think about the learning environment in a much broader way: "We recognize that an environment includes social, cultural, and psychological elements as well as physical features" (Hiemstra and Sisco, 1990, p. 245). Although my own perspective within this broader framework is still evolving, the present volume was conceived and negotiated as a means for compiling the thoughts of several colleagues on the topic of the learning environment. I believe that this volume will help adult educators expand their knowledge and reformulate and fine-tune their practices as related to learning environments. Certainly, my own thinking and approach to teaching have been influenced by the ideas presented here.

## Defining Learning Environments

Having described the initial impetus in my personal journey to a working definition of learning environments, I now want to clarify my current thoughts on the topic within this "broader" framework. The scope of my thinking is defined in part by the various aspects of learning environments that have already been examined by several scholars:

White (1972) has developed several criteria for assessing physical environments, and Vosko (1984) has looked at several microcomponents of physical spaces, such as seating arrangements and distance zones.

Hiemstra and Sisco (1990) have developed a checklist of items for analyzing the appropriateness of various physical environment components, centered on sensory concerns, seating, and furnishings.

Tagiuri (1968) has presented a taxonomy of environmental climate components, composed of ecology (building on classroom characteristics), milieu (individuals' characteristics), social system (interpersonal or group-patterned relationships), and culture (beliefs, values, and expectations).

Galbraith (1989, 1990) has suggested that the educational climate consists of both the physical environment and the psychological or emotional climate (for example, what takes place during the first session to establish a supportive, challenging, friendly, informal, and open atmosphere).

Pappas (1990) has laid out four key elements of what he calls the psychological environment, including spatial behavior, physical characteristics (light, temperature, noise, decor, and furniture arrangements), the role of tradition, and the affective experience (how a person anticipates and responds to a learning setting).

Belsheim (1986, 1988) has described organizational environments within continuing education settings in terms of culture, politics, economics, technological know-how, and geographical areas served.

David (1979) has called for alternative ways of conceptualizing the physical environment, defining a functional approach to the environment in which physical features and social and curricular concerns are soon to intersect.

Gibb (1978) has developed EQ, an environmental quality scale, for measuring trust relationships within an organizational context.

Fraser and Treagust have developed the College and University Classroom Environment Inventory (CUCEI) (Fraser and Treagust, 1986; Fraser, Williamson, and Tobin, 1987), used to measure what they call the psychosocial environment.

Darkenwald and Valentine (Darkenwald, 1989; Darkenwald and Valentine, 1986; Langenbach and Aagaard, 1990) have developed the Adult Classroom Environment Scale (ACES), used to measure the social environment of adult education classrooms.

Fellenz and Conti (1989, 1990) have clarified the need to better understand the social environment, including such issues as racism, discrimination, employment, and critical thinking, in relation to adult learning.

My personal journey and the reports cited above on the diverse ways that people view learning environments indicate the complexity of these environments. Recognition of this complexity has led me to formulate a much broader definition than I would have been capable of deriving only a few years ago. I offer the following definition, focused on the adult learner, as an indication of where I am now on my continuing journey: *A learning environment is all of the physical surroundings, psychological or emotional conditions, and social or cultural influences affecting the growth and development of an adult engaged in an educational enterprise.*

I have invited and organized contributors to this volume according to these several dimensions. No doubt my own view of this definition will broaden or at least change over time. Readers will have their own views on what should be included in, excluded from, or added to the definition. One of the volume contributors (Susan Collard, personal communication, December 1990), for example, wondered why I did not invite an author to write on the impact of social class on learning environments. Clearly, limits on space precluded consideration of many pertinent issues. For the issues we have addressed, I hope readers will consider engaging me, the other authors, and their own colleagues in discussions about this volume and the information contained within it.

## Ingrained Views of the Learning Environment

It has been my experience from numerous hours of talking about instruction and the learning environment with colleagues that there are many educators who do not want to think about the issues raised in this volume. Part of the problem is that many people fall back on or find comfort in what they already know, and some of the issues raised here are very complex and can cause painful self-reflection.

I hope that this volume serves to stimulate new attitudes and ideas, however discomforting the process, and leads to the development of more effective learning environments. There are at least three ways in which these changes can be brought about.

In the late 1970s, Mezirow (1978) introduced "perspective transformation" to adult educators. This concept, derived from earlier work (Mezirow, 1975), is based on the notion that in adult development an essential kind of learning involves "how we are caught up in our own history and are reliving it" (Mezirow, 1978, p. 101). Influenced by people such as Freire (1970), Gould (1978), and Habermas (1970, 1971), Mezirow suggests that learning is more than the accumulation of new knowledge, added on to existing knowledge; it is a process where many basic values and assumptions by which we operate are changed through our learning process.

Collard and Law (1989) provide a critique of Mezirow's work that warrants serious consideration (also see Mezirow, 1989), but my point in describing perspective transformation here is to illustrate the process of growth and development in relation to our knowledge about learning environments. If such knowledge is an accumulation of past knowledge and that accumulative collection does not include observations about critical social and psychological issues, then how can we expect to substantively inform our practice from the knowledge that does exist? In other words, a broader view of the learning environment begets more successful teaching and learning experiences. Thus, I hope that this volume promotes perspective transformations that increase our effectiveness as educators.

The second way of instigating positive change, and a way closely related to perspective transformation, involves paradigms and paradigm shifting. Our behaviors and attitudes are shaped by the paradigms we know, believe in, or have directly experienced. The word *paradigm* is usually associated with models, theories, frames of reference, or perceptions. In essence, our paradigms are the way we see, perceive, or understand the world around us. For example, my accumulated knowledge and experience in relation to learning environments—my paradigm or, more accurately, collection of paradigms—informs part of my view of myself as an adult educator, explains in part why I embrace the educational approaches that I use, and serves in part as the basis of my advocacy of the cause of improving our learning environments.

What is required of many people is a "paradigm shift." Knowles (1989) refers to this phenomenon as flashes of insight or episodes that can change a life. Kuhn (1970) introduced the notion of a paradigm shift by demonstrating how most significant advancements in scientific endeavors are the products of breaks with old or traditional ways of thinking. Covey (1989) describes how paradigms affect the way we think about or see things. I know that my own instructional approaches have changed through my paradigm shift to the broader view of learning environments described above.

The third way of achieving change is through knowledge of how personal philosophy affects ways of working with people. Elsewhere I have suggested that there are at least four reasons why an adult educator should be able to explicate a personal philosophy: "(1) A philosophy promotes an understanding of human relationships. (2) A philosophy sensitizes one to the various needs associated with positive human interactions. (3) A philosophy provides a framework for distinguishing, separating, and understanding personal values. (4) A philosophy promotes flexibility and consistency in working with adult learners" (Hiemstra, 1988, p. 179).

I contend that an individual's philosophy, whether it is explicated or not, affects personal instructional styles or approaches in various ways. Thus, I suggest another task for readers of this volume is to think about, analyze, and use their own respective philosophies: "Philosophy contributes to professionalism. Having a philosophic orientation separates the professional continuing educator from the paraprofessional in that professionals are aware of what they are doing and why they are doing it" (Merriam, 1982, pp. 90–91). I urge readers to explicate or reexamine their personal philosophies as adult educators and to see if their thinking about learning environments is as broad as that suggested in this volume.

## Conclusion

The journey to more effective learning environments begins with adult education practitioners making personal improvements in their understanding and practice. This may require changes that will be difficult to achieve. However, it is my hope that the following chapters prove helpful in promoting new knowledge and application skills related to working with adult learners.

## References

Becker, J. "Architecture for Adult Education." In M. Knowles (ed.), *Handbook of Adult Education in the United States*. Washington, D.C.: Adult Education Association of the U.S.A., 1960.

Belenky, M. F., Clinchy, N., Goldberger, L., and Tarule, J. M. *Women's Ways of Knowing: The Development of Self, Voice, and Mind*. New York: Basic Books, 1986.

Belsheim, D. J. "Organizing Continuing Professional Education." *Adult Education Quarterly*, 1986, *36*, 211–225.

Belsheim, D. J. "Environmental Determinants for Organizing Continuing Education Professional Education." *Adult Education Quarterly*, 1988, *38*, 63–74.

Brockett, R. G., and Hiemstra, R. *Self-Direction in Adult Learning: Perspectives on Theory, Research, and Practice*. London, England: Routledge & Kegan Paul, 1991.

Collard, S., and Law, M. "The Limits of Perspective Transformation: A Critique of Mezirow's Theory." *Adult Education Quarterly*, 1989, *39*, 99–107.

Commission on Architecture. *Architecture for Adult Education*. Chicago: Adult Education Association of the U.S.A., 1956.

Covey, S. R. *The Seven Habits of Highly Effective People: Restoring the Character Ethic*. New York: Simon & Schuster, 1989.

Damon, A., Stoudt, H., and McFarland, R. *The Human Body in Equipment Design*. Cambridge, Mass.: Harvard University Press, 1966.

Darkenwald, G. G. "Enhancing the Adult Classroom Environment." In E. R. Hayes (ed.), *Effective Teaching Styles*. New Directions for Adult and Continuing Education, no. 43. San Francisco: Jossey-Bass, 1989.

Darkenwald, G. G., and Valentine, T. "Measuring the Social Environment of Adult Education Classrooms." In *Proceedings of the 1986 Adult Education Research Conference*. Syracuse, N.Y.: Syracuse University Printing Services, 1986.

David, T. "Students' and Teachers' Reactions to Classroom Environment." Unpublished doctoral dissertation, University of Chicago, 1979.

Fellenz, R. A., and Conti, G. J. *Learning and Reality: Reflections on Trends in Adult Learning*. Information Series No. 336. Columbus: ERIC Clearinghouse on Adult, Career, and Vocational Education, Ohio State University, 1989.

Fellenz, R. A., and Conti, G. J. (eds.). *Social Environment and Adult Learning*. Bozeman: Center for Adult Learning Research, Montana State University, 1990.

Fraser, B. J., and Treagust, D. F. "Validity and Use of an Instrument for Assessing Classroom Psychosocial Environment in Higher Education." *Higher Education*, 1986, *15*, 37–57.

Fraser, B. J., Williamson, J. C., and Tobin, K. G. "Use of Classroom and School Climate Scales in Evaluating Alternative High Schools." *Teaching and Teacher Education,* 1987, *3,* 219–231.

Freire, P. *Pedagogy of the Oppressed.* New York: Herder and Herder, 1970.

Galbraith, M. W. "Essential Skills for the Facilitator of Adult Learning." *Lifelong Learning: An Omnibus of Practice and Research,* 1989, *12* (6), 10–13.

Galbraith, M. W. "Attributes and Skills of an Adult Educator." In M. W. Galbraith (ed.), *Adult Learning Methods.* Malabar, Fla.: Robert E. Krieger, 1990.

Gibb, J. R. *Trust: A New View of Personal and Organizational Development.* Los Angeles: Guild of Tutors Press, 1978.

Gilligan, C. *In a Different Voice: Psychological Theory and Women's Development.* Cambridge, Mass.: Harvard University Press, 1982.

Gould, R. L. *Transformations.* New York: Simon & Schuster, 1978.

Habermas, J. *Toward a Rational Society.* Boston: Beacon Press, 1970.

Habermas, J. *Knowledge and Human Interests.* Boston: Beacon Press, 1971.

Hayes, E. R. "Insights from Women's Experiences for Teaching and Learning." In E. R. Hayes (ed.), *Effective Teaching Styles.* New Directions for Adult and Continuing Education, no. 43. San Francisco: Jossey-Bass, 1989.

Hiemstra, R. "Creating a Climate for Adult Learners." Unpublished recommendations to the Management Training and Education Program, Lincoln General Hospital, Lincoln, Nebraska, 1976.

Hiemstra, R. "Translating Personal Values and Philosophy into Practical Action." In R. G. Brockett (ed.), *Ethical Issues in Adult Education.* New York: Teachers College Press, 1988.

Hiemstra, R., and Sisco, B. *Individualizing Instruction: Making Learning Personal, Empowering, and Successful.* San Francisco: Jossey-Bass, 1990.

Hugo, J. M. "Adult Education History and the Issue of Gender: Toward a Different History of Adult Education in America." *Adult Education Quarterly,* 1990, *41,* 1–16.

Hunsaker, H., and Pierce, R. *Creating a Climate for Adult Learning.* Chicago: Adult Education Association of the U.S.A., 1959.

Kemp, J. E. *Planning and Producing Audiovisual Materials.* (3rd ed.) New York: Crowell, 1968.

Knowles, M. S. *The Modern Practice of Adult Education.* New York: Association Press, 1970.

Knowles, M. S. *The Making of an Adult Educator: An Autobiographical Journey.* San Francisco: Jossey-Bass, 1989.

Kuhn, T. S. *The Structure of Scientific Revolutions.* (2nd ed.) Chicago: University of Chicago Press, 1970.

Langenbach, M., and Aagaard, L. "A Factor Analytic Study of the Adult Classroom Environment Scale." *Adult Education Quarterly,* 1990, *40,* 95–102.

Merriam, S. B. "Some Thoughts on the Relationship Between Theory and Practice." In S. B. Merriam (ed.), *Linking Philosophy and Practice.* New Directions for Adult and Continuing Education, no. 15. San Francisco: Jossey-Bass, 1982.

Mezirow, J. *Education for Perspective Transformation: Women's Re-Entry Programs in Community Colleges.* New York: Center for Adult Development, Teachers College, Columbia University, 1975.

Mezirow, J. "Perspective Transformation." *Adult Education,* 1978, *28,* 100–110.

Mezirow, J. "Transformation Theory and Social Action: A Response to Collard and Law." *Adult Education Quarterly,* 1989, *39,* 169–175.

Pappas, J. P. "Environmental Psychology of the Learning Sanctuary." In E. G. Simpson and C. E. Kasworm (eds.), *Revitalizing the Residential Conference Center Envi-*

*ronment.* New Directions for Adult and Continuing Education, no. 46. San Francisco: Jossey-Bass, 1990.

Sommer, R. *Personal Space.* Englewood Cliffs, N.J.: Prentice-Hall, 1969.

Tagiuri, R. "The Concept of Organizational Climate." In R. Tagiuri and G. H. Litwin (eds.), *Organizational Climate: Explorations of a Concept.* Boston: Division of Research, Graduate School of Business Administration, Harvard University, 1968.

Vosko, R. S. "The Reactions of Adult Learners to Selected Instructional Environments." Unpublished doctoral dissertation, Syracuse University, 1984.

Vosko, R. S., and Hiemstra, R. "The Adult Learning Environment: Importance of Physical Features." *International Journal of Lifelong Education,* 1988, 7, 185–195.

White, S. *Physical Criteria for Adult Learning Environments.* Washington, D.C.: Commission on Planning Adult Learning Systems, Facilities, and Environments, Adult Education Association of the U.S.A., 1972.

Woodson, W. E., and Conover, D. W. *Human Engineering Guide for Equipment Designers.* (2nd ed.) Berkeley and Los Angeles: University of California Press, 1966.

*Roger Hiemstra is professor of adult education and chair of the adult education graduate program at Syracuse University, Syracuse, New York.*

*The SPATIAL model offers educators a conceptualization of
the physical environment as a contributing factor to learner
participation, satisfaction, and achievement.*

# A Conceptual Model for Understanding the Physical Attributes of Learning Environments

*Rodney D. Fulton*

## Why Worry About the Physical Environment?

Considerable speculation about the relationship of learners to physical
environments has occurred during the past forty years. Unfortunately, too
little critical research on learning and physical environments has been
reported during this same period. While educational research has dealt
with many variables found to be important in the learning equation, practitioners have been relatively uninformed about either the potential value
or the possible harm of physical space to learning. These effects can be
seen not only in achievement levels, the traditional outcomes variable measured in educational research, but also in levels of participation and satisfaction. Participation is a critical variable in nonmandated education; thus,
the physical environment's impact on participation rates can be especially
important in educational and training efforts outside of school settings.

Since adults usually have more options than do children in dealing
with issues of satisfaction, the relationship of physical environment to
satisfaction in learning becomes a very germane question with adults. Many
researchers have attempted to establish and report the relationships of
space to learning. However, educators must often rely on studies in noned-
ucational settings such as hospitals, prisons, and offices. Much of this re-

The author acknowledges the contribution of Roger Hiemstra to the development
and naming of the SPATIAL model.

search conceptualizes the relationships from an architectural point of view. Other information is found in psychological frameworks, workplace training, aesthetics, sociology, and human factors engineering. Even when the relationships of a setting's physical attributes to learning have been considered within an educational framework, findings frequently have been limited to children and may or may not be applicable to adults.

While a body of knowledge does exist that documents the relationships between learning and physical environment, there are problems that need to be resolved before the present level of understanding can be systematically advanced. One problem is that common vocabulary does not exist. Thus, in the literature, concepts are often described with similar but not identical terminology. Conversely, the same terms are used for similar but not exactly the same concepts. But this confusion in vocabulary is only a symptom of the fundamental problem: the lack of a conceptual model that explores relationships of physical environment to learning rather than to behavior in general. Architectural models address built environments, emphasizing both interior and exterior features of building design that allow, encourage, prohibit, or inhibit various behaviors. Psychological models discuss environmental attributes that set conditions for or even control human behavior. Sociological models emphasize the importance of environment in terms of how it facilitates human interactions. By emphasizing individual appreciation of the environment, aesthetic models address the relationship of values to human behavior. Workplace training models, including human factors engineering, emphasize the fit between environment and person and seek out optimal conditions for performance.

Each of these perspectives can add to a global understanding of the learning environment; however, a model that addresses learners in learning environments is a needed first step in refining educational research. The model described here—satisfaction-participation-achievement-transcendent/immanent attributes-authority-layout (SPATIAL)—can serve as a fundamental basis for organizing research designed to identify relationships between and among components of the learning environment and attributes of the learner. Further, this model has potential for weaving together findings from architectural, psychological, sociological, aesthetic, and human factors engineering studies.

Not only is there a need to know more about the physical attributes of learning environments, but adult educators must also develop an organizational schema for understanding the research findings. Perhaps Vosko and Hiemstra's (1988, p. 186) assertion that "physical features appear to have been primarily ignored in the adult education literature" is true not because little is known but rather because little of what is known is understood within a larger conceptual framework.

## Some Underlying Assumptions

Commonly held assumptions about the physical environment need to be critically examined. First, the proposed model, SPATIAL, challenges the assumption that physical arrangement is only important for how it enhances or detracts from social interaction. Physical environment along with psychological, sociocultural, and instructional environments need to be viewed as important in their own right as well as in relation to the others. Weinstein (1981, p. 12) relegated physical environment as "clearly secondary in importance." However, SPATIAL establishes no hierarchy among environments.

A very common research method has been to investigate some particular aspect of physical environment and draw conclusions based on the relationship of one or two discrete variables to learning. David (1979) challenged this approach and suggested that it would be more meaningful to consider the interrelation of physical features and instructional activities in what he labeled a functional approach to the environment. SPATIAL is based on such a functional approach; it looks at no single physical attribute without also considering how that attribute is related to the functioning of the learning environment.

The physical environment is defined by both material attributes and the perceptions of those attributes by learners. Two examples can clarify this distinction. Density can be measured as square footage per occupant in a room, but crowding is a measure of how a person defines available personal space. Temperature is readily measured in degrees, but thermal comfort is a subjective evaluation by an individual. Thus, a place can have high density but be rated as crowded by one group and not crowded by another, or a certain room temperature can be considered cool by some and warm by others. Attempts to address physical attributes of learning must acknowledge these simultaneous realities of material and perceived attributes.

Finally, the SPATIAL model does not suggest that there can, or even should, be a perfect physical environment for all learning. As Hiemstra and Sisco (1990, p. 259) expressed, "Is it possible to satisfy everyone's needs? Probably not!" This model allows for a dynamic tension among its component parts that can be used by adult learners, facilitators, and future researchers to maximize the impact of interaction among several attributes of the functional physical environment. This interaction creates several possibilities rather than one desired or best physical environment.

## Selected Literature on Physical Environment

The critical thought needed to build an adequate model of the physical environment is enhanced by familiarity with the current literature. Knowing what has been written allows one to question assumptions, understand limits, and propose new relationships. While space is limited, I offer a brief review of literature selected for its contribution to the SPATIAL model (see Fulton and Hiemstra, this volume, for an annotated bibliography of additional sources).

Organizational training environments are a major research interest and have been well reported in the literature. Propst (1974, p. 609) has summarized one problem in the study of physical environments: "How well do we know the school or the workplace? They have suffered from being too close and too familiar—literally under our noses, within sight and touch. Little attention has been paid to the physical environment because of overfamiliarity with its overt characteristics but also because of the tendency of physical arrangements to static formality. There is also a widespread assumption that physical settings have little impact on organizational functioning."

In the early 1970s, the concept of office landscape became prominent, especially in German studies. Brooks and Kaplan (1972, p. 373) assumed that "there is evidence that the physical environment does affect human behavior and perception." Viewing the person as a part of the environment, Goulette (1970, p. 40) claimed that "consideration of these differences [among individuals] by the instructor will inevitably result in happier and more satisfied students." Swor (1987, p. 92) claimed that "trainers and meeting planners need to consider the overall impression a facility makes on participants—both inside and outside the meeting room. The environment created by the sum of these subjective design considerations either helps or hinders the ultimate goal: successful meetings." Finkel (1984, p. 32) called for "learning-engineered" environments because "if we specify the environment completely enough, we can predict human behavior exactly."

Learning styles also have been analyzed in relation to the physical environment. Golay (1982) called for a balance between classroom design and instructional activity to increase student achievement. Dunn and Dunn (1978) proposed a theory that includes environmental, emotional, sociological, and physical stimuli as elements of learning style. Environmental stimuli are exterior to the person and include sound, light, temperature, and design. Physical stimuli are seen as internal and include perceptions (per the five human senses), intake, time, and mobility. Dunn, Beaudry, and Klavas (1989, p. 50) have claimed that "studies conducted during the last decade have found that students' achievement increases when teaching methods match their learning styles." Those methods include important environmental factors that are often overlooked in educational planning.

Several studies, both in higher education settings and in primary and secondary schools, have established a relationship between place or space and learning. In stating that "the physical arrangement of most college classrooms reveals much about the learning process" (Becker, Sommer, Bee, and Oxley, 1973, p. 514), the authors concluded that "our data support the notion that simply altering the physical structure, without an accompanying change in the social structure, will not produce real change" (p. 523). In a Canadian study, Gifford (1976) found that communicative behavior was adversely affected by negative feelings derived from the inhospitable physical attributes of the college classroom. Wollin and Montagne (1981, p. 713) found that "the background of an interaction between a teacher and student can have a strong effect on the quality of that interaction."

Studies presenting data on how individuals conceptualize the physical environment can help us build models. Getzels (1974, p. 529) offered four types of classroom designs that correspond to four "different beliefs and conceptions—the visions—of the child as learner." The rectangular classroom of the turn of the century was for the empty learner. The square classroom with moveable furnishings served the active learner. The circular classroom with opportunity for interpersonal interaction supported the social learner. Finally, the open classroom, which appears at times to be chaotic and sensory-enriched, facilitated the stimulus-seeking learner.

In declaring that "little systematic attention has been paid to the role that the physical environment (the built or constructed environment) might play in the process of instruction," David (1979, p. 1) noted that "environments don't *teach* per se, and it is unlikely that variations in physical setting alone within broadly defined limits of human tolerance should have a significant impact on student achievement (although some investigators have sought to establish such a link)." Studies that actually have focused on changes in learning behaviors when physical environment attributes were modified are often inconclusive or contradictory. If David's concerns are correct, this ambiguity is to be expected. As Johnson (1973, p. 1) has described, "The relationship between the physical, the social, and the psychological factors that make the total environment and the extent to which the single variables that compromise each of these factors bear upon the total matrix of a class is less than clear. One reason for this lack of clarity stems from the general tendency of educators to ignore or outright reject the role the environment might play in the dynamics of learning or teaching."

The appearance of the "open school" led Proshansky and Wolfe (1974, p. 557) to state that "the crucial issue is the relationship between the philosophy of education and how the physical setting can be used to implement that philosophy. They suggested that the physical design offers a "symbolic message of what one expects to happen in a particular place" (p. 558). McVey (1971, p. 5) outlined how sensory factors were important to school learning environments, observing that "traditionally, teachers have depended upon their own common sense observations of how sensory stimuli work in the learning environment. Some of the research findings . . . confirm such observations; other findings provide new information and insights."

The adult education literature has paid only brief attention to the relationship of physical setting to learning. In the 1950s and 1960s, certain members of the Adult Education Association of the United States of America were actively investigating this relationship. White, for example, (1972) saw one-fourth of learning as dependent on the facility. Later, Hiemstra (1976) viewed the environment as important to the task of sustaining the learner's commitment. Vosko (1984) concluded from a review of the literature that while physical environment does affect activity and productivity, how it does so depends on the learners' perceptions. Concern for the older learner and the physiological changes of aging have led some adult educators to recommend changes in the physical environment to compensate for learner deficiencies (Borthwick, 1983; Verner and Davison, 1971).

Often the physical environment is presented as one of many tools that an educator can manipulate in instructional design. Looking at the physical environment from an administrative point of view, Lane and Lewis (1971, p. 97) acknowledged that "requirements for physical facilities for an adult learning laboratory will vary with the purpose of the laboratory, its organizational affiliation, and the availability of space." Lane and Lewis (1971, pp. 91–92) also assumed that "adults are more likely to be influenced by their surroundings than children and their motivation may be increased through adequate space, appealing decoration, and useable furnishings." Langerman (1974, p. 43) emphasized the physical environment as one of several components of a total learning environment: "Of no little importance and perhaps the first component to be considered is the physical environment."

This brief literature review supports the concept that the physical environment is an important element in instructional activity. However, neither learning nor physical environment is a single-sided concept. Both have multiple dimensions that must be understood holistically in order to capture the true nature of the relationship of physical space to learning.

## SPATIAL Model

In attempting to synthesize prior research findings in order to develop a new conceptual model for understanding the physical environment in learning, I realized that the model must allow for multiple types of learning environments; it can not just apply to classrooms. The model also must address the complex nature of relationships between physical settings and learning activities by allowing for interaction among several variables, including both the physical dimensions of a space as instructional variables and the multidimensional outcomes of learning. The SPATIAL model is a preliminary effort to better understand the physical environment and the complex interactions with learning activities. It accomplishes this task by hypothesizing that (1) individual perceptions of space affect learner satisfaction, participation, and achievement; (2) certain aspects of a space, as perceived by learners, are subjective or beyond the visible physical attributes; and (3) authority and layout are external realities that can be changed. The SPATIAL model thus establishes three levels at which to consider the relationship of physical environment to learning, thereby serving as a tool for future study and discussion.

**Learning as Satisfaction, Participation, and Achievement.** The first level defines learning. For design clarity, studies often measure learning in terms of some single dimension of achievement. However, the SPATIAL model defines learning as three-dimensional. *Satisfaction* is an intrinsic measure of how pleased or fulfilled a learner is with an activity. *Participation* is a measure of how engaged a learner is with an activity. For example, both physical presence and time-on-task can be measures of participation. *Achievement* is a measure of progress toward one or more learning goals. These three dimensions are seen as interrelated, and although they can be measured individually, all need to be assessed when measuring learning.

Physical attributes can affect the three learning dimensions simultaneously, yet in opposite directions. For instance, a particular seating arrangement may increase satisfaction but may decrease participation if a certain learner wants to remain relatively anonymous in a new setting. Or a multisensory presentation may increase achievement while decreasing a person's satisfaction if a nonpreferred learning style is engaged. Thus, the educator must always bear in mind the potential enhancement and detraction from learning that any changes to the physical environment can simultaneously enact.

**Transcendent and Immanent Attributes.** The second level in the SPATIAL model addresses reality. Several of the studies reviewed earlier here, and many that were not, deal with aspects of the physical environment that transcend the individual learner's control. Temperature, lighting, density, noise levels, and seating arrangements are all objective realities of the setting. These attributes normally exist independently of any particular individual, and each can be measured objectively on some scale. However, many studies have established that these realities are tempered by the immanent perceptions of humans in the environment. The processing of stimuli into perceptions adds environmental components that are subjective and unique to each individual.

Thus, both the *transcendent* and *immanent* attributes of the setting are, by this account, in healthy tension with each other. Educators of adults need to address these two realities in educational planning. For example, the facilitator should ensure that transcendent attributes such as furnishings, space, lighting, and ventilation are examined and altered if necessary. However, activities such as environmental analysis and visualization in which participants focus on their own evaluations of the environment can be used to address immanent perceptions of physical space.

**Authority and Layout of the Physical Environment.** The third level of the SPATIAL model addresses the nature or locus of control. *Authority* is one of the messages of the physical environment. That is, the power of learners to assess the adequacy of a place and to change attributes of the physical environment varies across settings. For example, an environment can be authoritarian or institutionalized in nature, affording learners little power for change, as when windows are sealed shut or when heating is automatically turned off at a certain hour. On the other hand, some aspects of an environment are within a learner's control, such as movable and adjustable furnishings. The relationship of authority to physical environment is very much contingent on the educational philosophy and purposes of an instructor and on whether or not learners are encouraged to take more control of their own environments.

*Layout* of the learning environment causes the many structural attributes of a place. Heating, ventilation, air conditioning, type of lighting, furniture, audiovisual equipment, and the human bodies occupying the space are all part of the layout. But also included are learning purposes, which determine many physical dimension requirements. For instance, Vosko (1984) describes how a sociopetal seating arrangement (a semicircular seating arrangement that facilitates face-to-face sightlines among learners) enhances participation when discussion is the purpose.

When layout alone is examined, as has too often been the case, the question of how a learning environment is controlled is often ignored. The interrelationship of authority and layout allows for a more complete understanding of how a particular educational setting might be perceived by certain learners. Knowles (1980) told the story of a program's failure to attract students because the building smelled too much like a school to potential adult learners, suggesting that they recalled earlier times when they had little power to affect change or control aspects of the physical layouts of their learning environments.

## Ideas for Practice

Use of the SPATIAL model to understand the relationship of physical environment to learning means that adult educators can examine the appropriateness of a learning situation in various ways. Emphasis can be placed on the structural reality as well as on individuals' perceptions of those realities. Thus, if nothing can be done to change a particular attribute, attention can be given to altering individuals' perceptions of it. For example, if a room has a high density, the task is to transform feelings of crowdedness into feelings of closeness and cooperation among the learners. In most settings, individuals' expressed needs for personal space can help the group interact more effectively through mutual respect of these space requirements.

The components of this model also allow practitioners several potential avenues for improving adult learning; they permit researchers to delineate the variables being studied in new ways. But both practitioners and researchers must bear in mind that the total effect of the learning place cannot be understood by any one single SPATIAL component. In this model the whole is truly greater than the sum of its parts. Thus, the model encourages qualitative analysis of several interactions, as informed by assessments of component parts. Several questions that educators and learners can address are shown in Exhibit 1. The reader is challenged to add to the list.

## Exhibit 1. Checklist for Addressing SPATIAL Needs

*Satisfaction, Participation, and Achievement*

_____ 1. Have learners been asked how satisfied they are with the space being used?

_____ 2. Have distracting physical features been removed or eliminated whenever possible?

_____ 3. Do learners stay on task in the setting that is provided?

_____ 4. Does body language indicate a desire to leave?

_____ 5. Does the place allow learners to use appropriate learning strategies?

_____ 6. Can auditory, tactile, and visual learning styles be used?

*Transcendent and Immanent*

_____ 7. Are the location and room size appropriate for the planned learning activities?

_____ 8. Do the furnishings "fit" the people who will be using them?

_____ 9. What messages about learning could be assumed by the learners from the condition of the space?

_____ 10. Is there potential for some individuals to be challenged or offended by some aspect of the space?

*Authority and Layout*

_____ 11. Can changes be made in the learning environment?

_____ 12. Who can make changes?

_____ 13. Does the space meet minimal safety and comfort standards?

_____ 14. Are necessary special requirements such as appropriate audiovisual equipment available?

# References

Becker, F., Sommer, R., Bee, J., and Oxley, B. "College Classroom Ecology." *Sociometry*, 1973, *36*, 514–525.

Borthwick, T. *Educational Programs and the Older Adult.* Davis: Experiential Learning Project, University of California at Davis, 1983.

Brooks, M., and Kaplan, A. "The Office Environment: Space Planning and Affective Behavior." *Human Factors*, 1972, *14*, 373–391.

David, T. "Students' and Teachers' Reactions to Classroom Environment." Unpublished doctoral dissertation, University of Chicago, 1979.

Dunn, R., Beaudry, J., and Klavas, A. "Survey of Research on Learning Styles." *Educational Leadership*, 1989, *46* (6), 50–58.

Dunn, R., and Dunn, K. *Teaching Students Through Their Individual Learning Styles: A Practical Approach.* Reston, Va.: Reston, 1978.

Finkel, C. "Where Learning Happens." *Training and Development Journal*, 1984, *38* (4), 32–36.

Getzels, J. "Images of the Classroom and Visions of the Learner." *School Review*, 1974, *82*, 527–540.

Gifford, R. "Environmental Numbness in the Classroom." *Journal of Experimental Education*, 1976, *44* (3), 4–7.

Golay, K. *Learning Patterns and Temperament Styles.* Newport Beach, Calif.: Manas-Systems, 1982.

Goulette, G. "Physical Factors to Consider When Training Adults." *Training and Development Journal*, 1970, *24* (7), 40–43.

Hiemstra, R. "Creating a Climate for Adult Learners." Unpublished recommendations to the Management Training and Education Program, Lincoln General Hospital, Lincoln, Nebraska, 1976.

Hiemstra, R., and Sisco, B. R. *Individualizing Instruction: Making Learning Personal, Empowering, and Successful.* San Francisco: Jossey-Bass, 1990.

Johnson, R. "The Effects of Four Modified Elements of a Classroom's Physical Environment on the Social-Psychological Environment of a Class." Unpublished doctoral dissertation, Oregon State University, 1973.

Knowles, M. S. *The Modern Practice of Adult Education: From Pedagogy to Andragogy.* (Rev ed.) New York: Cambridge University Press, 1980.

Lane, C., and Lewis, R. *Guidelines for Establishing and Operating an Adult Learning Laboratory.* Raleigh: North Carolina State University School of Education, 1971.

Langerman, P. (ed.). *You Can Be a Successful Teacher of Adults.* Washington, D.C.: National Association for Public Continuing and Adult Education, 1974.

McVey, G. *Sensory Factors in the School Learning Environment: What Research Says to the Teacher.* National Education Association Report, series no. 35. Washington, D.C.: National Education Association, 1971.

Propst, R. "Human Needs and Working Places." *School Review,* 1974, *82,* 608–616.

Proshansky, E., and Wolfe, M. "The Physical Setting and Open Education." *School Review,* 1974, *82,* 556–574.

Swor, J. "Site Design: Meeting of the Minds." *Training,* 1987, *24* (12), 89–92.

Verner, C., and Davison, C. *Physiological Factors in Adult Learning and Instruction.* Tallahassee: Research Information Processing Center, Department of Adult Education, Florida State University, 1971.

Vosko, R. S. "Shaping Spaces for Lifelong Learning." *Lifelong Learning,* 1984, *9* (1), 4–7, 28.

Vosko, R. S., and Hiemstra, R. "The Adult Learning Environment: Importance of Physical Features." *International Journal of Lifelong Education,* 1988, *7,* 185–195.

Weinstein, C. "Classroom Design as an External Condition for Learning." *Educational Technology,* 1981, *21,* 12–19.

White, S. *Physical Criteria for Adult Learning Environments.* Washington, D.C.: Commission on Planning Adult Learning Systems, Facilities, and Environments, Adult Education Association of the U.S.A., 1972.

Wollin, D., and Montagne, M. "College Classroom Environment: Effects of Sterility Versus Amiability on Student and Teacher Performance." *Environment and Behavior,* 1981, *13,* 707–716.

*Rodney D. Fulton holds master's degrees in psychology and adult and higher education. He is adjunct instructor in the Department of Education and staff member in the College of Nursing, Montana State University, Bozeman. During much of the past three years he has explored the physical environment in learning.*

*Spaces for adult learning experiences are shaped by administrators, teachers, maintenance personnel, and even learners. The way these physical environments are arranged and manipulated can affect learning experiences.*

# Where We Learn Shapes Our Learning

*Richard S. Vosko*

I sometimes wonder if I should have signed up for this. What a day this has been. I overslept and forgot to make the kids' lunch. I got to work ten minutes late. There never seems to be enough time to talk with my children. Tonight the baby sitter was late and now I'll be late. Where is that building anyway? Gee, it's so dark along these walkways. "Excuse me, how can I get to the lecture hall?" Ah, there it is. No signs anywhere. Let's see, I want Room 408B. Darn, wouldn't you know it, the room is on the top floor and there's no elevator. Gosh, I can't seem to find a bathroom here. Finally, there's the classroom. Wow, what a big class and only that empty seat in the middle of the last row left. "Excuse me, please!" My, what a small chair. I'll just put my coat here on the floor. Oops, it's too dirty so I'll just put it over my shoulder. Seems a little chilly in here anyway. What's that on the board and where are my glasses?

The vignette above reads like a worst-case scenario. But so many adults who return to the classroom do not lead well-ordered and neatly arranged lives. Mahoney (this volume) describes many pieces of personal, emotional, psychological, and external baggage that learners can be carrying around. The person in my story, a male, is a single parent who is trying to keep a job, raise a family, and earn a degree all at the same time. He is ready to learn and has an urgent need to earn a degree. But, his responsibilities are very demanding and create all sorts of pressures for him. I remember when I returned to the classroom while continuing my self-employed job as a consultant. There were so many times when I just could not keep my mind on a course's subject matter. Frequently, even the act of going to school was a burden to me. In my vignette, the man had a pressure-filled day and arrived at the class in a state of disarray. What he did not need at that time were more hassles, but he encountered many space-related inconveniences: poor lighting, lack of signage, no security, difficult access, remote toilets, small classroom, small seats, crowding, poor sightlines, cool temperature, and little work space.

In this chapter I describe, first, what I do as a space specialist. Second, I make some general observations about what I have learned from my work. Third, I address four factors that can affect adult learning situations. Finally, I offer some conclusions and suggestions for creating or manipulating physical settings to achieve environments conducive to learning.

## My Work as a Space Specialist

As a designer and consultant in the building and renovating of places of worship, I am an agent of change who makes connections between ever-developing religious traditions and practices and their effects on the places where people worship. My initial training for this profession was largely in the fields of theology, art, and architecture. After many years of working with adults, I realized that I needed to know more about the way in which adults learn, so I secured additional training in adult education. After all, I was trying to help people create new physical settings to accommodate new worship practices. There have been similar shifts in the creation of physical settings for adult learning programs (Hiemstra, 1976; Vosko, 1984) in efforts to facilitate the learning experience (Hiemstra and Sisco, 1990; Knowles, 1980). Throughout this chapter I compare the creation of effective worship spaces for religious groups with the creation of effective learning spaces for adults.

While learning about adult education techniques and methods, I established a process based on adult education models to assist people in learning more about space issues and how to articulate their specific space needs and expectations. I begin by helping the people develop a plan that is very similar to a learning contract. Our goal together is to create the best possible place for particular worship activities, social affairs, and educational programs.

One of the most successful components of this process is similar to the "instructional audit" described by Hiemstra and Sisco (1990, p. 56). I take the planners of religious spaces on tours of the architectural spaces in which learning and worship activities occur so that we can "audit" or examine various environmental factors. I ask the people to examine the space that we are touring and to note how they feel about colors, decorative materials, lighting, and temperature and whether or not the place makes them feel welcome.

Such tours inevitably reveal how much we adults do not pay attention to the physical spaces in which we live and work. This is true for many reasons. Some people are not problem solvers; they are simply unaware of their feelings or blind to the impact of their surroundings. Other people may lack knowledge about their environments and, therefore, are unable to express their feelings. For some adults, physical space issues may be a marginal concern. For others, the space is fine just the way it is. Still others might say, "Gosh, I never noticed that before." My point is that the built environment affects our behavior whether we notice it or not. Research on office environments and building designs has focused on this question of how worker productivity can be affected by the work environment (Becker, 1982; Pappas, 1990; Steele and Jenks, 1977).

In my work I have learned that the worship space, usually shaped by only a few people (clergy and architects), affects worship practices of the entire congregation. If the way in which a house of worship or office building is designed affects the patterns of adult behavior, it is reasonable to posit that a direct relationship between variables of physical space and behavior exists as well in places where adults gather to learn.

## Observations from My Work

Across hundreds of diverse settings I have observed that there are kindred relationships between people and places that sometimes defy explanation. At least three categories for such relationships are evident.

**People Are More Important Than Buildings.** An early Christian writer named John of Chrysostom said that it is not the building that makes the people holy; rather, it is the people who come into the building who make the church holy. In other words, it is the people who give meaning to their buildings. I can recall standing in a Russian Orthodox church in Paris on Good Friday several years ago, watching the people embrace each other and shake hands even while the worship service was being conducted. It was as if the human connection was more important than the divine. For these people, the presence of friends was a very important part of the worship experience. These recollections have helped me work with my clients in developing hospitable gathering areas in their buildings where they can meet and greet each other before, during, and after their worship services.

My own experience as an adult learner showed me the value of such camaraderie. Often, the tension of going to school and working at the same time was bearable only because of friendships I established with teachers and other learners. Even though gathering places and lounges were not always conveniently located where we went to school, we somehow managed to mingle and engage in conversation. It made my learning experience more humane. In fact, the act of going to school with other adults was just as important as what I learned. What could have enhanced this experience was a building that respected us foremost as human beings.

**Hospitality: An Essential Building Material.** Although humans can adapt and survive in the most austere conditions, the physical environment should foster friendliness. I have observed that places of worship that appear inhospitable are often used by people who do not seem to care about each other.

For example, I have noticed that barrier-free accessibility for physically challenged persons is not always conveniently available, especially *inside* religious buildings. Once a person gets into the space, it is frequently difficult for that individual to be mobile throughout the interior. Handrails, textured directions embedded in the floors, and braille markings on the walls aid the visually impaired person. When I asked about the lack of such amenities in one congregation, I was told, "We don't have any of those handicapped people here!" Buildings that are user-friendly are places that reflect people who are hospitable. They make sure that the environment is pleasing and welcoming.

There is a corollary point here from my observations. A building cannot be any more hospitable than the people who use it. No matter how well equipped or designed a facility may be, there really is no substitute for friendliness and hospitality among users of the facility. In religious buildings, hospitality is a word that turns value systems into actions. In reality, hospitality should be a watchword in all adult learning settings.

**Teachers and Learners Working Together.** In a previous age, religious rituals were the sole responsibility of the clergy. And in the classroom the lesson plan was the domain of the teacher only. Today, clergy are not so much dispensers of spiritual goods as they are enablers. Their job is to involve people in affairs of the congregation. The clergy have thus had to learn new leadership methods. One of their tasks now is to take advantage of the life experiences of congregational members. Clergy are expected to foster environments of mutuality and collaboration among members. The worship space should reflect this change in function.

So, too, the adult teacher is more than a dispenser of knowledge, and in learning situations he or she should try to create an ambiance that encourages hospitality and inclusivity. The two tasks of taking care of the learning environment and looking after each other's welfare are related. For example, if I respect someone as a human being, I will do my part in making that person comfortable when near me. I believe that places of worship and learning have this mutual courtesy in common. Both spaces are more hospitable when we are more thoughtful in dealing with each other.

## Factors Affecting Adult Learning Situations

An administrator from a congregation on the West Coast recently told me that once the offices in their church were renovated and redecorated, it seemed that the congregation became more active; the place was busier.

Similarly, I believe a teaching environment that is well tended breeds more active participation in the learning experience. There are many factors in the built environment that can affect adult behavior (Burgess, 1981; Huchingson, 1981; Paradise and Cooney, 1980), four of which I consider here.

**Territoriality.** I have learned from talking with worshipers that many like to sit on the outside perimeter of a congregational space. They do so for different reasons. Some adults do not want to get too close to clergy who represent authority and divinity. Other adults suffer from claustrophobia and need to sit near exits and away from crowds.

Human creatures, like other creatures, tend to establish territories. Adjustment of things in our personal spaces is another of our interesting habits. We do this to give meaning to our space and to create a sense of comfort or familiarity (Ashcraft, 1976; Insel and Lindgren, 1978). When someone encroaches on our space we tend to become defensive and protective. To use a chicken-and-barnyard metaphor, there is a pecking order in human society. It is described in terms of rich and poor, educated and uneducated, powerful and weak, and so on.

For example, traditionally in religious settings nonordained persons (members of the congregation) do not walk or sit with ordained persons (the clergy). Some people enjoy this distinction or privilege, while others despise it. It creates psychological and social walls that are reflected in physical barriers such as rails, chancels, and sanctuaries in churches. As another example, barriers are used in courts of law to create a hierarchy of persons (the judge, the judged, the jury, the guards, and the spectators). Whether it is the amount of land on which we live or the space that is designated ours in the church or classroom, territoriality is a physical factor that can alter behavior (Sommer, 1969, 1974).

Personal space needs and territoriality in instructional settings can be dealt with by making sure that the spaces are not overcrowded and that each adult has adequate space for working and for storing personal items. Further, any barriers that are physical should be dismantled if the teacher wants to convey an atmosphere of collaboration in the learning experience. For example, sitting behind a large desk on a platform, a teacher could be perceived as the fount of all knowledge, inaccessible and even indifferent to students' experiences. Care also must be taken to honor the territoriality needs of adults. One adult learner told me that he sits in the row farthest away from the teacher so that he will not be called on. Another learner once spoke of an uneasiness when the teacher paced the floor nearby that student's seat.

**Seating Arrangements.** Traditionally, religious buildings are thought of as long, narrow edifices that have unmovable, straight rows of seats grouped together so that congregations face the platform where clergy conduct the worship service. Newer places of worship have discovered a different spatial attitude that is more inviting, one that encourages active participation in the ritual activity and discourages the social stratification mentioned above.

"Sociofugal" (Hall, 1974; Osmond, 1959) seating arrangements are those that focus on a single person, object, or action. This arrangement expects no interaction among those seated together. It discourages involvement in the action witnessed. Cinemas and older, larger lecture halls are usually arranged in this fashion. All of the attention is on either the screen or the teacher. There are times when such undivided attention on an image is required, and the best seating arrangement for viewing the image is linear rows. But adult learning experiences depend on more than just presentations by teachers or projections of images on a screen. At the heart of many classrooms is the interaction that takes place among learners or among the teacher and learners. In this case, "sociopetal" or semicircular (Hall, 1974; Osmond, 1959) seating arrangements are more appropriate. This pattern not only allows for participation in the learning activity but also encourages interaction among learners.

Depending on enrollment, the best situation is to provide a room that has flexible furnishings. This flexibility enable users to rearrange the space to accommodate a variety of learning activities. There are times when one seating pattern is more useful than another.

**Sightlines.** There is another good reason for a semicircular seating arrangement, especially for large groups: sightlines. A semicircular pattern brings more people closer to the heart of the teaching action (Hall, 1959, 1966). For example, I have observed that in a church that seats one thousand people in long straight rows, the last row can be as much as 120 feet away from the front, depending on the building width. However, in a semicircular arrangement of one thousand seats, no one ever is more than 60 feet away from the front. The latter arrangement creates much better sightlines, not only in churches but also in classrooms.

Based on my experience, in order to provide good sightlines in large instructional settings, the teacher should be elevated six to seven inches for every fifteen feet of distance away from a learner. When the slope of the floor is one foot of rise for every twelve feet of length, the platform's elevation need not be proportionately high. Although physical elevation of the teacher can create better sightlines for learners, an elevated platform can suggest a hierarchy in the learning place, one in which the teacher is presented as the only source of knowledge in the room. Further, instructional settings with sloped floors should be barrier-free, allowing physically challenged persons to sit where they wish. While sloped floors are more friendly than flat surfaces, movable seats cannot be used on them. So even though stepped classrooms are designed to provide good sightlines for large groups, the seats cannot be rearranged.

Visual field is an important ingredient in the sightline issue. When a learner is seated, the teacher or focal point should fall within a visual field that is thirty degrees off the center axis. That is, as I look straight forward I should not have to twist my body and head or move my eyes to the left or right beyond thirty degrees, otherwise anthropometric discomfort is created (Vosko, 1984). For this reason swivel seats are useful in large instructional halls. The best solution, however, is to encourage smaller learning groups where learners can gather in more informal settings that still provide essential furnishings and materials for the learning activity.

**Equipment.** We live in a time that is being shaped dramatically by the ubiquitous presence of electronic media and computers in our work and domestic environments (see DeJoy, this volume). I wonder if, in this age, there can be an effective adult learning environment without this orientation toward electronic media and computers.

I recently attended a two-day workshop on new software programs for my computer system. In each class the lecturer presented the information using a keypad and a mouse. The colorful images were projected onto a very large, easy-to-read screen. Although we were seated in straight rows facing the screen, a sociofugal arrangement, there was still an interactive feeling in the group. I wondered if I was being drawn into a new kind of learning experience or, because I am a product of the television generation, was I comfortable because I was looking at information flowing across a television-like screen. I learned a lot in that class in a very short period of time because of how the presenter manipulated and presented information using the computer. Further, because the information was presented so concisely and orderly, there was ample time in the program for interaction with the teacher and other learners. I am not yet sure what the related implications are for adult instructional settings, or even for places of worship. However, we should probably pay attention to what many change agents have known for a long time: Adult teachers must never stop being adult learners.

Newer and refurbished instructional settings are often equipped with built-in provisions for projected media. Many places of learning even have staffs or teacher aides who set up and operate the equipment. All that remains for the teacher is to design courses that take advantage of such technology.

## Conclusion

I have learned from many religious leaders, and from my own observations in the field, that members of congregations do not always arrive for worship on time. Further, when they do arrive, they expect the place to look good and the minister and choir to be prepared to present a meaningful program. The man in my opening vignette rushes to class after a harrowing day because he needs to get a degree in order to survive. This may not be the case for other adult learners who return to school with a more leisurely agenda. Every learner is different. However, in most adult education programs, learners expect that someone will be ready to facilitate something worthwhile in a place of learning that will be pleasant. It is still the adult facilitator or teacher who makes the class a good or bad experience.

I suggest that there are several things adult teachers can do to prepare an adequate space for the learning experience. Although Hiemstra and Sisco (1990, p. 85) provide a checklist "for analyzing the appropriateness of a learning setting for adult learners," I have a somewhat different set of items, as follows. Moreover, in Exhibit 1 I provide a checklist that the teacher can use to carry out a space audit.

### Exhibit 1. Analysis of Space Attributes

*Outside the Classroom*
_____ 1. Clear signage showing identification and direction
_____ 2. Barrier-free access along walkways and in the building
_____ 3. Adequate lighting for safety and security
_____ 4. Availability of coatrooms, restrooms, student lounges, and vending machines
_____ 5. Location of emergency exits and clear directions to them

*Inside the Classroom*
_____ 6. Adequate lighting for evening classes
_____ 7. Availability of emergency lights
_____ 8. Cleanliness of classroom
_____ 9. Barrier-free accessibility to and in the classroom
_____ 10. Classroom painted with cheerful colors
_____ 11. Windows and blinds or shades that are operable
_____ 12. Adequate control over ventilation, heating, and cooling
_____ 13. Flexible furnishings
_____ 14. Available media equipment
_____ 15. Adequate sightlines for everyone in the classroom

*Rearrangement of the Classroom*
_____ 16. Familiarize yourself with the space. Walk all around the room. Notice how it feels in different locations.
_____ 17. Set up the room to suit your needs as a teacher.
_____ 18. Explore the options to suit class members' needs.
_____ 19. Try to imagine which arrangement will work best for which learning activity.
_____ 20. Check for sightlines, glare, lighting, crowding, access, and work space convenience in each arrangement.

*Miscellaneous*
_____ 21. Search for another classroom if yours is not right.
_____ 22. Conduct a space needs assessment with the learners.
_____ 23. Invite the learners to help rearrange the space.
_____ 24. Encourage comfort and friendliness.
_____ 25. Do a formative evaluation of the space performance.
_____ 26. Do a summative evaluation for the administration.
_____ 27. Thank the learners for helping create the instructional environment.

*Do a Space Needs Assessment.* We all have opinions about space. Not all of us can articulate them clearly, but we do have them. A good time to find out about spatial preferences is during the needs assessment component of any course. During this time the teacher could ask about temperature (Do some like it hot? Do some like it cold?), crowding (Is this room too small or large?), seat comfort and work space (How many have taught in places where the seats were designed for younger bodies?), sightlines (Can everyone see?), and, in larger rooms, acoustics (Can everyone hear?). The learners could also add a listing of their own space-related needs.

*Extend an Invitation to Get Comfortable.* This may sound a little too risky to some teachers. Nevertheless, it is really a way of saying, "I am glad you are here; we are all adults with valuable experiences to share; no one of us knows more than all of us; I am here to enable you to learn more about this topic, so let's get comfortable and go to work." Most adults will like this approach, although a few may feel that the instructor should just teach and not worry about comfort.

*Be Sensitive to Quiet Learners.* Some adults never let the teacher know anything more about them than that they have signed up for the course. Yet, they have space needs as well as learning needs. Once the teacher recognizes such a person, a more personal approach concerning the instructional setting might be helpful. The teacher may have to identify the "quiet learners" and wait for an appropriate time to approach them. An alternative method is to prepare a written form so that learners can indicate their respective space needs.

*Regularly Check for Space-Related Problems.* Periodically during the course pause to discuss the instructional setting and determine if space-related needs are being met and how further improvements can be made. This kind of formative evaluation is helpful in sustaining a friendly space.

I have learned that the perfect place for worship has not yet been built, probably because the worshiping community is not yet perfect. Nevertheless, work directed toward the creation of appropriate religious buildings is ever-developing. The same thought applies to adult learning settings. Many of us experience places of learning that are far from perfect. As the practice of adult education continues to develop, many teachers are becoming more proficient. New research in the field of adult education continues to inform and challenge us. Increased attention to the physical environment for learning can help us appreciate that where we learn shapes our learning.

## References

Ashcraft, N. *People Space: The Making and Breaking of Human Boundaries.* Garden City, N.Y.: Anchor, 1976.

Becker, F. D. *The Successful Office: How to Create a Workspace That's Right for You.* Reading, Mass.: Addison-Wesley, 1982.

Burgess, J. H. *Human Factors in Built Environments.* Newtonville, Mass.: Environmental Design and Research Center, 1981.

Hall, E. T. *The Silent Language.* Garden City, N.Y.: Doubleday, 1959.

Hall, E. T. *The Hidden Dimension.* Garden City, N.Y.: Doubleday, 1966.

Hall, E. T. *Handbook for Proxemic Research.* Washington, D.C.: Society for the Anthropology of Visual Communications, 1974.

Hiemstra, R. "Creating a Climate for Adult Learners." Unpublished recommendations to the Management Training and Education Program, Lincoln General Hospital, Lincoln, Nebraska, 1976.

Hiemstra, R., and Sisco, B. *Individualizing Instruction: Making Learning Personal, Empowering, and Successful.* San Francisco: Jossey-Bass, 1990.

Huchingson, R. D. *New Horizons for Human Factors in Design.* New York: McGraw-Hill, 1981.

Insel, P. M., and Lindgren, H. C. *Too Close for Comfort: The Psychology of Crowding.* Englewood Cliffs, N.J.: Prentice-Hall, 1978.

Knowles, M. S. *The Modern Practice of Adult Education: From Pedagogy to Andragogy.* (Rev. ed.) New York: Cambridge University Press, 1980.

Osmond, H. "The Relationship Between Architect and Psychiatrist." In C. Goshen (ed.), *Psychiatric Architecture.* Washington, D.C.: American Psychiatric Association, 1959.

Pappas, J. P. "Environmental Psychology of the Learning Sanctuary." In E. G. Simpson, Jr., and C. E. Kasworm (eds.), *Revitalizing the Residential Conference Center Environment.* New Directions for Adult and Continuing Education, no. 46. San Francisco: Jossey-Bass, 1990.

Paradise, R. C., and Cooney, N. L. "Methods for Assessments of Environments." In L. Krasner (ed.), *Environmental Design and Human Behavior.* Elmsford, N.Y.: Pergamon Press, 1980.

Sommer, R. *Personal Space.* Englewood Cliffs, N.J.: Prentice-Hall, 1969.

Sommer, R. *Tight Spaces: Hard Architecture and How to Humanize It.* Englewood Cliffs, N.J.: Prentice-Hall, 1974.

Steele, F., and Jenks, S. *The Feel of the Work Place.* Reading, Mass.: Addison-Wesley, 1977.

Vosko, R. S. "The Reactions of Adult Learners to Selected Instructional Environments." Unpublished doctoral dissertation, Syracuse University, 1984.

*Richard S. Vosko is an independent designer and consultant for worship environments, serving communities throughout North America. He works out of his studio in Clifton Park, New York.*

*To see microcomputer technology from the adult learner's point*
*of view requires adult educators to understand how learners'*
*emotions, perceptions, and self-concepts affect the learning process*
*and to deal with instructional design and delivery issues.*

# Incorporating Microcomputer Technology into Adult Learning Environments

*Judith K. DeJoy*

With rapid technological improvements in the past ten years and a shift toward "personal" computer power (Smart and Reinhardt, 1990), microcomputer technology is now becoming part of adult learning environments. In this chapter, the term *microcomputer technology* is used to describe microcomputers and related peripherals in the service of specific instructional goals, with a focus on microcomputers and supporting equipment rather than a concern with the entire range of telecommunications technology.

Both in the business and educational communities, "The new . . . computers bring many necessary features of a powerful and sophisticated computer to the desk of the individual" (Mis, 1990, p. 83). The developments that put such "power" on an individual user's desk have also shifted the focus of adult education from learning *about* computers in order to program, to learning the skills necessary to work *with* computers (Heermann, 1986a). Adult educators and professional trainers are keenly aware of the accelerating pace of new information in all areas of adult life and how microcomputer technology is involved in access to that information. To truly work with computers, however, adults must first understand the basic concepts, be comfortable using software, and be able to critically analyze computer-based outcomes (Gerver, 1984).

The microcomputer is also recognized "as an educational delivery system . . . of particular value in continuing education because it provides a very flexible learning approach" (Bork, 1980, p. 79). In this context, the issues involved in incorporating microcomputer technology into adult learning environments take on a special priority.

## Thinking About the Issues

The issues discussed here relate both to the "nuts and bolts" involved in building microcomputer technology into adult learning environments and to what can be called the "human element" in microcomputer-assisted learning processes. These two categories include generic issues in the microcomputer-based learning environment, such as software, hardware, and staff, and *core* issues involved in the adult teaching and learning process. These core issues represent an internal structure, the sociopsychological context of adult learners, which must be recognized in order to create effective learning environments.

**Generic Issues.** These nuts-and-bolts issues include the following: (1) learning objectives appropriate to the technology, (2) suitable instructional materials, (3) equipment (hardware) requirements, (4) design and furnishings, (5) policies and daily procedures, and (6) staffing. The exciting pace of computer-technology development encourages the application of this technology to *all* learning experiences. Heermann (1986b), however, has suggested that the microcomputer as a teaching machine is best equipped to deliver information that is clear and well defined. Content areas such as management skills and interpersonal relations skills continue to require additional instructional components such as opportunity for interaction, guidance from instructors, and opportunity to practice. Technical skills training can incorporate microcomputer technology at the level of drills, tutorials, in-depth teaching programs, assessments, and testing (the concept of the "teaching machine"), as well as provide professional software for particular purposes (the concept of the "computer as a tool"), as Heermann (1986b, p. 9) also has discussed.

While a typing class, for example, could depend almost exclusively on computer-assisted instruction for skills training, work with self-instructional software programs in an ethics course would need to be incorporated into group discussions with an instructor's guidance. For example, individual student assessments and feedback from work with a software program on ethics case studies could be used as a basis for group discussion of ethical complexities and of various perspectives on ethical decision making.

Identification of suitable instructional materials is at the heart of these nuts-and-bolts considerations. While good self-instructional software programs cannot, alone, create appropriate learning environments, poor software programs can sabotage an otherwise excellent learning experience. Methods for locating and evaluating instructional software have been the topic of countless articles and many books during the past fifteen years. Not all recommendations, however, include the critical step of identifying characteristics of the target student populations. This identification is important to the selection of potential instructional materials that match learners' interests, levels of knowledge, and degrees of computer experience.

The next phase, evaluating these potential materials, entails exploration of the materials on a preview basis and use of objective criteria for evaluation. Based on experiences with adult learners using microcomputer-based instruction, DeJoy and Mills (1989) developed a set of evaluation criteria that now guide software purchases for the University of Georgia Personal Adult Learning Lab. These five evaluation categories include the following: accuracy and applicability of content, instructional strategies, instructional presentation, documentation of operation steps, and technical aspects, each with a set of specific guidelines. Any evaluation tool, however, can only serve as a general guide for decision making; a more definitive strategy is to solicit adult student volunteers who are representative of the target student population to work with a particular instructional program and help identify potential problems. Small details can make a difference. For example, adult learners with even limited computer experience respond to a self-paced software program differently from adult learners who have never seen a keyboard of *any* kind.

Reality often dictates the purchase of microcomputer equipment before instructional software programs are acquired; therefore, instructional software must be carefully evaluated for compatibility with existing technology. The importance of evaluation extends to the subsequent management of these instructional materials once they have been incorporated into the learning environment. This extra evaluation is needed because software documentation is not standardized and many differences exist in the operation of software programs.

Typically, choices in microcomputer equipment are guided by several factors, such as available funding, requirements of current instructional software (if any), and availability of similar hardware in the future (Hollowood, 1986). In addition, microcomputer hardware purchased today should be compatible with future refinements in data bases and distance education communications. It is also increasingly more difficult to become, and remain, a microcomputer "expert," in the strict sense of the word; but it is possible to become knowledgeable about the fundamental characteristics of microcomputer-based instructional delivery. In making decisions about whether to network microcomputers and how many printers to purchase, educators need to consider whether there is a need for learners to communicate with each other and the instructor, to work individually or as teams, and to have access to printed feedback. Once this level of planning has been completed, adult educators should use a computer expert (homegrown or imported) who can understand the specific educational goals and translate them into hardware requirements within the constraints of budget and available space.

The incorporation of microcomputer technology into the physical design of learning environments is usually subject to available funding, physical space limitations, and existing facilities. The number of computer systems required depends on the characteristics of the learning environment; for example, the extent to which adult learners will work with self-instructional programs or work as a group using class demonstrations will dictate the minimum number of computer systems required. Flexible arrangements using movable partitions and furniture will permit the physical design to be modified to meet specific instructional objectives. This will permit each learning station (desk, chair, microcomputer system) to vary in size, from a minimum of about fourteen to sixteen square feet to an optimal thirty-two to thirty-six square feet (Hollowood, 1986), depending on the need for writing spaces and for students to work in teams.

More important than the sheer number of computer systems is the scheduling of access to these instructional systems. Fewer systems are needed when access is very flexible, including evening and, perhaps, weekend hours. Hollowood (1986) has suggested that there is no single pattern of scheduling for adult student populations, which supports the need for flexible hours and the use of scheduled appointments in order to predict staffing needs. Permanent loading of software programs on individual microcomputers can also facilitate the daily operation and assist the staff.

The role of the staff, including the instructor, in bringing microcomputer technology into adult learning environments is critical because individual staff members manipulate instructional materials, hardware, the physical environment, and individual schedules to support successful learning experiences. Moreover, to be effective, these professional staff must possess a well-developed perspective on the adult learner in a computer-based learning environment and a sensitivity to some of the psychological and emotional components involved in the teaching and learning process, as discussed elsewhere in this volume.

**Core Issues.** These issues deal with the variables critical to "bridging the gap" between microcomputer technology and the individual adult learner. They include the learners' past experiences, emotions, perceptions, motivations, and self-concepts and their emotional responses to technology-oriented learning environments.

The issue of past experiences refers not only to the type of prior exposure the adult learner has had to microcomputers but also to the much more significant *lack* of any experience with microcomputer technology. When there is no prior experience with microcomputers, the learning experience is without precedent for adult learners, that is, individuals do not have personal images of themselves as successful learners with microcomputers. In addition, adult learners often bring to such a situation myths and half-truths about microcomputer technology that interfere with their initial learning, including notions about power and control in computer operations that more reflect science fiction than reality. An adult student wondering "which key balances my checkbook?" will need help in learning about the structure of basic computer commands and operations. Many software programs are described as "requiring little, if any, experience with computers." This description ignores the fact that an adult learner's relative (or absolute) lack of computer experience often represents a set of expectations, half-truths, fears, and so on that, if left unchecked, can sabotage the learning experience with even the "friendliest" software programs and computer systems.

Initial contact with the novel experience of working with computers can result in a variety of emotional responses, primarily negative. In addition, many adults pursuing new learning are also engaged in some type of transition (change in life events or experiences) that evokes emotional responses (Schlossberg, Lynch, and Chickering, 1989). These kinds of significant life changes include such experiences as the death of a spouse, divorce, job displacement, and job promotion. Learning objectives are often characterized by the need to learn and change quickly, in response to such real-life pressures. For example, one adult learner, Ellen, age forty-five, needed to learn about word processing to keep up with the others in the office; Harriet, a new widow at sixty-two, wanted to "do something easier than manual labor"; and George, retired at fifty-four due to ill health, planned to learn about desktop publishing in order to help advertise his wife's new business. The teaching and learning process for many adults in a microcomputer-based learning environment is thus intimately influenced by personal composites of past experiences, perceptions, and self-concepts, as well as by individual emotional responses at the two levels of personal life transitions and of demands for new or different learning skills necessary for learning success.

The importance of adult emotions has been underrepresented in our understanding of adult learning processes. Taylor (1988) has called this deficiency one of the "missing pieces" in our analyses of adult learning. Hiemstra and Sisco (1990, p. 31), in discussing barriers to educational participation, suggest a reason for this deficiency. They list three barriers—situational, institutional, and dispositional—and point out that while the first two are most often given as reasons for not participating in adult education programs, the real importance of dispositional factors [such as attitude or self-image limitations] is probably underestimated in that it is far more acceptable to say we are too busy to participate . . . than . . . to say we are too old to learn or lack the ability." The combined experience of life transitions and a completely unfamiliar learning environment demands significant coping skills for adult learners and specific facilitation skills for instructors.

The emphasis of this section is not on the technical and organizational skills of professional staff but rather on the role of the "educator as facilitator."

In order to successfully facilitate the teaching and learning process in a micro-computer-based learning environment, staff need to be sensitive to the strong psychological and emotional components at work and to utilize the following skills in their interactions with learners: (1) acknowledgment of and respect for the learners' perceptions, emotions, self-images, and motivations, (2) sensitivity to the "spoken" and the "unspoken," and (3) authentic encouragement and support of the individual learning process, including changes in self-awareness. Moreover, no single microcomputer-based teaching strategy and no single self-paced software program can meet the needs of all adult learners in the same way. Rather, different delivery formats are required for different learners and, possibly, for the same learners at different times during the teaching and learning process.

## Incorporating Microcomputer Technology into Adult Learning Environments

The actual development of microcomputer-supported adult learning environments can take a wide variety of forms, depending on particular instructional objectives, administrative constraints, funding, the range of instructional materials available, the degree of technical support, and the instructor's personal commitment. One of the most realistic approaches entails a combination of group and individual instruction options, which provides needed support to individual learners through microcomputer-based technology *while* learners continue to interact through group exercises and discussion.

Sheckley (1986) talks about the incorporation of microcomputer technology into adult learning environments in terms of innovative teaching and learning concepts, attitudes of trust toward adult learners, and the blending of high-technology and high-touch approaches involving significant instructor support and attention. Examples of how microcomputer technology can be blended into effective learning environments are the following: (1) skills instruction, using peer teams at the computer, (2) individual practice sessions following skill training, (3) demonstrations to large groups, (4) specific course content tutorials to supplement classroom activities, (5) work with specific application programs in developing projects, creating data bases, and developing graphics presentations, (6) access to online data base resources for individual projects, (7) individual learner study tracks, based on sets of self-paced instructional software programs, and (8) use of self-assessment materials for personal learning.

A checklist can serve as a guide for adult educators who are considering ways of integrating microcomputer technology into adult learning environments. The following directives are pertinent to generic issues: (1) Carefully consider those program learning objectives that can be better achieved with microcomputer-based instruction. Is the curriculum involved clearly defined? Could students benefit from individualized practice or decision making? Can appropriate software be identified? (2) Identify and evaluate instructional materials for potential use. Is appropriate software available? Does the content meet documented learning needs? Is the degree of difficulty matched to target students? Does the software meet objective evaluation criteria? Is the software compatible with current hardware? (3) Identify the microcomputer hardware necessary to support delivery of instructional software. Is the hardware compatible with available instructional software? Can the hardware be upgraded? Is the computer hardware competitively priced? Are maintenance and technical support provided? (4) Plan for the physical design and daily operation of microcomputer-based instruction programs. Are learning stations available for individual learning activities? Are there sufficient numbers of microcomputers? Is there a scheduling plan? Are instructions for operating instructional programs available to staff? Are sufficient staff available to provide individualized assistance? Are all staff adequately trained in the software and hardware operations?

The following directives are pertinent to core issues: (1) Ensure that all staff can help adult learners develop accurate perceptions of the learning process and appropriate learning skills. Do all learners appreciate that there is *no* age limit on learning? Do all learners believe that anxiety is normal? Do all learners appreciate that individual learning styles are positive? Do learners have basic reading, writing, and math skills? Do learners possess a degree of self-awareness about their personal biases, strengths, and attitudes? (2) Ensure that all staff possess the critical facilitation skills required to identify, acknowledge, and support the adult learner's past experiences and emotional responses during the teaching and learning process. Do staff practice active listening skills, such as paying attention, empathy, and reflection? Are staff able to encourage learners' efforts by using genuine praise, providing acceptance, and encouraging independent problem solving? Can staff adequately discriminate learners' feelings and respond appropriately?

## Conclusion

If microcomputer-based instruction and the various innovative educational strategies that it supports are actually changing the nature of the teaching and learning process, interactions between adult learners and computers will require new learning perspectives. Lewis (1989, p. 626) has developed a lengthy "to do" list for adult educators trying to integrate microcomputers into learning environments; no single educator could implement all of these recommendations. However, the final one, "meeting the needs of individuals while . . . seeing to it that learners are central to the process," is critical to the field and best implemented by adult educators because it embraces the "educational relationship" between technology and adult learners. What is required is a commitment to mediate these interactions with adult learners as the starting point.

## References

Bork, A. "Computers in Continuing Education." In M. N. Chamberlain (ed.), *Providing Continuing Education by Media and Technology.* New Directions for Adult and Continuing Education, no. 5. San Francisco: Jossey-Bass, 1980.

DeJoy, J. K., and Mills, H. H. "Criteria for Evaluating Interactive Instructional Materials for Adult Self-Directed Learners." *Educational Technology,* 1989, 29 (2), 39–41.

Gerver, E. *Computers and Adult Learning.* Milton Keynes, England: Open University Press, 1984.

Heermann, B. (ed.). *Personal Computers and the Adult Learner.* New Directions for Adult and Continuing Education, no. 29. San Francisco: Jossey-Bass, 1986a.

Heermann, B. "Strategies for Adult Computer Learning." In B. Heermann (ed.), *Personal Computers and the Adult Learner.* New Directions for Adult and Continuing Education, no. 29. San Francisco: Jossey-Bass, 1986b.

Hiemstra, R., and Sisco, B. *Individualizing Instruction: Making Learning Personal, Empowering, and Successful.* San Francisco: Jossey-Bass, 1990.

Hollowood, J. R. "Designing Microcomputer Facilities for Continuing Education." In B. Heermann (ed.), *Personal Computers and the Adult Learner.* New Directions for Adult and Continuing Education, no. 29. San Francisco: Jossey-Bass, 1986.

Lewis, L. H. "New Educational Technologies for the Future." In S. B. Merriam and P. M. Cunningham (eds.), *Handbook of Adult and Continuing Education.* San Francisco: Jossey-Bass, 1989.

Mis, F. W. "Computer-Assisted Instruction." In I. M. Hefzallah (ed.), *The New Learning and Telecommunications Technologies.* Springfield, Ill.: Thomas, 1990.

Schlossberg, N. K., Lynch, A. Q., and Chickering, A. W. *Improving Higher Education Environments for Adults: Responsive Programs and Services from Entry to Departure.* San Francisco: Jossey-Bass, 1989.

Sheckley, B. G. "Microcomputers and Adult Learning: Maximizing Potentials." In B. Heermann (ed.), *Personal Computers and the Adult Learner.* New Directions for Adult and Continuing Education, no. 29. San Francisco: Jossey-Bass, 1986.

Smart, G., and Reinhardt, A. "1975–1990: 15 Years of Bits, Bytes, and Other Great Moments." *Byte,* 1990, 15 (9), 369–400.

Taylor, M. "Self-Directed Learning: More than Meets the Observer's Eye." In D. Boud and Y. Griffin (eds.), *Appreciating Adults Learning: From the Learners' Perspective.* London: Kogan Page, 1988.

*Judith K. DeJoy is coordinator of the Personal Adult Learning Lab, a microcomputer-based adult learning environment, at the Georgia Center for Continuing Education, University of Georgia, Athens.*

*The process of teaching and learning success begins during the first encounter between instructor and students and develops thereafter.*

# Setting the Climate for Effective Teaching and Learning

*Burton R. Sisco*

Mary White had just returned from an exhilarating night at her local community college where she had begun a course on "Life Work Planning." She had been away from school for nearly twenty years, and after raising two children and surviving an unpleasant divorce, she was looking forward to starting a career in retail sales. Years before, her father had been a successful clothier in the small town where she grew up, and during summers she worked in the store. Mary had many fond memories of this experience and hoped to one day start her own clothing business. But before doing so, she needed to learn more about operating a small business and developing a business plan.

Several weeks earlier, Mary had been discussing her plans with a friend who suggested that she contact the career-planning office of the local community college for assistance. Mary was pleased to learn of a new small business certificate program that sounded good. But before jumping in, the counselor suggested she take the "Life Work Planning" course as a way of clarifying her goals and building confidence.

Now that the first class session was over, Mary could hardly restrain herself. Many good things had happened during the evening. She thought how neat the other twelve students were and how competent and caring the instructor seemed to be. She was impressed by how quickly the time went, noting that two and one-half hours is a long time to sit, but a short break was included in the middle of the session. She also recalled how her initial anxiety gave way to calm as she learned about the other participants and their reasons for taking the course. The instructor had made her feel comfortable and confident that her life experiences were of value. "Yes,"

Mary said to herself, "I think I'm going to enjoy this class and the people in it. I'm glad the counselor suggested I take it first. I can't wait for our next meeting!"

Most instructors would be elated to have someone like Mary in class since she seems so enthusiastic and ready to learn. She represents the epitome of a motivated learner, the kind often idealized in adult education literature. But a closer reading of Mary's story reveals certain anxieties associated with the teaching and learning process that, left unchecked, could make the difference between success and failure for teacher and student alike. There are thousands of adults like Mary who approach a new course or workshop with varying degrees of anxiety. For some, the thought of returning to school after a long interruption may cause physical or psychological pain as they wonder whether they can still learn and keep up. For others who have been frequent participants in continuing professional education activities, the pressure of balancing work responsibilities and academic assignments may lead to personality changes.

Successful instructors are aware of the wide range of anxieties that adults bring to the classroom and make an effort to deal with them early. They realize that the first session is crucial to the eventual success of that undertaking. By creating a climate in which each participant can feel comfortable, secure, and able to learn, they have created the conditions for successful teaching and learning.

This chapter addresses the importance of climate setting as a means for enhancing the teaching and learning environment. Particular emphasis is placed on the importance of the first time an instructor meets with learners and how this can ensure subsequent success in the teaching and learning process. Such issues as planning for the first session, using icebreakers, and monitoring the learning environment are discussed. Finally, a model for organizing the first session's work is described, followed by concluding comments.

## Climate Setting Defined

Most of us have a fairly good idea of what the term *climate* means. With respect to a geographical place or region, climate refers to the typical weather patterns based on time of the year. But climate can carry another connotation such as a prevailing condition, atmosphere, or ambiance; this meaning is the chapter's focus in the context of teaching and learning, particularly with adults.

A few years ago, Apps (1985, 1989) described a process of helping teachers and other adult educators analyze what it is they do. An early part of this analysis involves critical examination of the assumptions we make about our role as teachers and of those we make about the nature and role of our adult students and the teaching-learning transaction. Apps used metaphors to help participants clarify their assumptions about the teaching and learning process. For example, two instructors offering the same noncredit workshop on financial planning at the local night school can operate very differently. The first instructor organizes and teaches the class along fairly traditional lines. The syllabus is clearly laid out with course objectives described in performance terms. The main teaching technique is a lecture, participants are seated in five rows, and the instructor uses only personal examples rather than selecting examples from the group.

In contrast, the second instructor has a syllabus, but this is contained in a workbook along with other items such as learning activity descriptions, suggested course objectives, and related reading materials. The seating pattern of the class is semicircular ("sociopetal," as defined by Vosko, this volume), so each participant can see one another, and the instructor can have small groups working on a common learning activity. Clearly, the two instructors are engaging learners and operationalizing the teaching-learning transaction in different ways.

Thinking metaphorically, how can we describe the methods by which the two instructors teach the financial planning course? The first instructor is following the learner-as-machine metaphor. This instructor uses a prescriptive teaching approach and encourages a passive role for learners. In contrast, the second instructor sees the teaching-learning transaction as an opportunity for learners to grow and develop using personal experience. Learners are encouraged to relate their experience to the course content with the instructor serving as a process facilitator. In this situation, the appropriate metaphor might be learner-as-flower, noting the developmental emphasis implicit in the experience.

The process of climate setting can also be analyzed metaphorically, since it makes a number of assumptions regarding adults as learners and regarding the aims of educators and their beliefs about content and process and the teaching-learning transaction (Apps, 1989). In this chapter, climate setting is used as a metaphor for effective teaching, particularly with adults. This approach is based on the notion that adults are mature individuals who want to be treated as such. They tend to be diverse in nature, owing to the breadth of their experiences, and have a nascent need to direct their own learning. Because of these conditions, it is important for instructors to create climates early in the learning experience that not only acknowledge such assumptions about adults but also enable the assumptions to surface in the teaching and learning process.

Other adult education writers agree with this posture and support the idea of climate setting, although different terminology may be used. One of the best-known advocates of climate setting is Knowles (1980), who sees it as tantamount to helping people learn. He specifically uses the term *educative environment* as analogous to climate setting to describe those conditions that promote the growth and development of adults. These conditions include "(1) respect for personality; (2) participation in decision making; (3) freedom of expression and availability of information; and (4) mutuality of responsibility in defining goals, planning and conducting activities, and evaluating" (Knowles, 1980, p. 67).

Another advocate for climate setting is Knox (1986), who focuses on the task of building supportive and active learning environments, especially during the first session. While acknowledging that some adults resist active participation because of its excessive effort, responsibility, and risk, most actually thrive under such conditions if they are supported and challenged early. Knox (1986, pp. 132–134) suggests a number of ways that an instructor can create a supportive and challenging setting, especially during the first session: choose attractive facilities that participants are likely to find hospitable and comfortable, help participants get acquainted with each other, present oneself as a person, reduce apprehension by using icebreakers or warm-up activities that reflect empathy and learner advocacy, encourage active participation by having participants introduce themselves, provide an overview of the course or workshop content, obtain feedback from participants about their initial reactions, encourage the return to the learning experience by emphasizing success, be available for informal conversation, review and summarize the first session, and provide an advance organizer of what will occur during the next class session.

Still another supporter of climate setting is Brookfield (1990), who believes that the building of trust is essential for meaningful learning. He identifies a number of characteristics that make instructors more trustworthy in the eyes of students, including teacher credibility and authenticity. According to Brookfield (1990, pp. 163–164), "Teacher credibility refers to teachers' ability to present themselves as people with something to offer students. When teachers have this credibility, students see them as possessing a breadth of knowledge, depth of insight, and length of experience that far exceeds the students' own." Teacher authenticity consists of (1) being explicit about how the teaching and learning experience is to be organized and the evaluative criteria used, (2) making sure one's words and actions as an instructor are consistent and congruent, (3) being ready to admit errors, (4) revealing aspects of oneself as a person outside an instructor's role, (5) taking students seriously by listening carefully to their concerns, anxieties, or problems, and (6) realizing the power of role modeling. All of these tasks must be done with care and consistency. As Brookfield (1990, p. 176) says, "Teaching is never easy, and of all the complex balances we try to attain, being credible and authentic in the right proportions is one of the most difficult." Successful climate setting aids such critical balancing during the first session.

## Preparing to Meet with Learners

There are actually many decisions to be made and activities to be planned before the first meeting with learners. One of the first is development of a rationale statement that describes the learning experience's purposes, the instructional process, and how and why the experience will contribute to personal as well as professional development. Other activities include identification of desired learning competencies, determination of associated requirements, and acquisition of necessary learning resources such as books, articles, and audiovisual materials.

A useful device for organizing the various learning materials is a workbook or study guide. Here, many of the learning materials can be assembled, such as the course, workshop, or training syllabus; descriptions of suggested requirements; bibliographical citations; simulations, case studies, or skill-based learning activities; and special readings. An important advantage of creating a workbook or study guide is that it helps facilitate advanced planning and preparation for the various learning experiences to come. It also serves as an initial resource for both instructors and learners to update as needed. On a personal level, the workbook or study guide helps learners obtain a broad picture of the learning experience, and many appreciate having materials assembled in one convenient package.

## Creating a Positive Learning Environment

Having completed any necessary preplanning activities, the next step is to establish a positive learning environment during the initial meeting with learners. Once again, there are a number of activities that often happen during the first few hours that an instructor and learners are together.

**Initial Contact with Learners.** Adults enroll in courses and workshops for a variety of reasons. Some enroll to update skills, others enroll for social reasons, while still others attend to address specific problems (Pratt, 1984). Whatever the reasons, it is important for an instructor to set a positive tone during the first session, since this is the time when learners form personal attitudes about the subject, the instructor, and the instructional process (Hiemstra and Sisco, 1990). The hope is that each learner leaves the first session with the same enthusiasm as did Mary White in the opening vignette. But her reaction was not accidental; it resulted from a deliberate attempt by an instructor to set a positive tone.

What are some of the activities that an instructor can pursue to create a positive environment? One of the first is to arrange the physical classroom space so that it is conducive to teaching and learning. It is recommended that the instructor arrive at least thirty minutes before class time so that the room can be made more comfortable and inviting for adult learners. This task often involves rearranging chairs in a semicircle or around a conference table so that all participants can see each other, adjusting the room temperature to a comfortable level, making sure that any audiovisual equipment is operating and visible at a distance, checking the chalkboard for chalk, and seeing that the lighting is adjusted properly.

Another suggestion is to bring along a hot pot to heat water for tea, coffee, and hot chocolate as well as assorted snacks for use during a break midway through the session.

Once participants start arriving, a warm, personal greeting is always welcome. Handshakes and self-introductions are nice touches as they help set an informal tone and give the instructor some idea about who is in attendance. Adults generally appreciate these gestures, even if some are shy and reserved.

**Creating the Three R's.** After participants have arrived and are seated comfortably, the major activities for the first session begin. Learners are going to have many questions, feelings, and thoughts as the instructor calls the session to order, all of which become opportunities for positive climate setting if handled properly. An especially good way of beginning is to address the following three key questions during the first session (Sisco, 1987):

*"Who Are We?"* Asking this question and even summarizing learners' responses are good ways of helping learners get to know one another and realize that they share many of the same questions and feelings. The question and responses also help to start the process of working together and creating a relaxed, informal environment.

*"Who Am I as the Instructor?"* In asking and answering this question, an instructor can establish credibility and authenticity with learners by indicating his or her qualifications to lead the educational experience. A particularly productive way of answering is to describe one's educational and experiential background. This is also a good time to share personal beliefs about what constitutes good and bad instruction and how this course or workshop will be a positive learning experience, even though there may be a good deal of personal challenge involved.

*"Why Are We Here?"* This question is a good lead-in to describing the general focus of the educational experience by touching on the overall content, suggested objectives, and instructional process. Also, any important housekeeping items can be discussed, such as attendance requirements, breaks, location of restrooms, and policies on food, refreshments, and smoking.

By taking time to address these questions, an instructor can help participants develop three types of relationships—the three R's—that are important in any classroom experience (Hiemstra and Sisco, 1990): (1) relationships with other class members, many of whom become valuable resources, support givers, and close friends, (2) relationships with the instructor, built on mutual trust, respect, and credibility, and (3) relationships with the content, material, and resources of the course or workshop.

Each of the three types of relationships normally exists to some extent in any class setting; however, two of them are typically overlooked or not even considered by many instructors. Often, emphasis is placed on the content or material of the educational experience with little attention directed to class members and the instructor. Any mention of goals, expectations, and learning activities is made almost incidentally, if at all. Very often learners may even be discouraged from asking pertinent questions about their backgrounds or potential roles in the learning experience. Good instructors of adults realize the value of climate setting and create a balance by encouraging establishment of these three types of relationships during the first class session.

**Using Icebreakers.** Icebreakers are techniques used at the beginning of the first session to reduce tension and anxiety, help acquaint participants with each other, foster involvement of all class members, and assist the instructor in getting to know class members and their range of experiences (Draves, 1984). They are very effective tools for initiating the three R's and can take many forms. The following are five icebreakers that all take less than an hour to complete, depending on the class size.

*Self-Introductions.* Participants introduce themselves and give reasons why they are attending the course or workshop.

*Partner Introductions.* Divide the group into pairs. A short interview is conducted by one partner of the other partner for five to ten minutes, then the roles are reversed. Partners then introduce each other to the entire group.

*Name Chain.* Participants introduce themselves one at a time to the group, each by saying his or her name and an adjective that begins with the same letter as the name. Each person in the chain must repeat all previous names and descriptors.

*Six Critters.* Display six different signs around the classroom, each with one of these words: owl, ostrich, rhinoceros, chameleon, fox, or lamb. Ask each participant to select the sign that best describes his or her dominant personality style. Divide participants into groups by the critter chosen and have group members introduce each other and list their critter's qualities. Then ask a recorder from each group to report the findings to the large group.

*Character Descriptions.* Have participants write down on pieces of paper their favorite foods, television programs, celebrities, animals, and musical artists. Then, one by one, have the participants relate these descriptions to the group and give their names. Be sure they explain the reasons for each choice.

There are many other icebreakers that instructors can use. Instructors should experiment with different types and even create their own variations.

**Monitoring the Learning Environment.** As the first class session unfolds, it is important to ensure that the learning environment remains positive. Be sure that the physical space remains comfortable and inviting by monitoring the room temperature so that it does not get too cold or hot. Observe the level of participation, noting that as the session progresses participants should become more involved in the proceedings. Periodically, use reinforcing statements that emphasize one's understanding of the anxiety that many people may face as they return to the classroom and one's commitment to everyone's success. These kinds of statements can bolster credibility and trustworthiness as an instructor. Finally, make sure that each participant leaves the first session, as Mary White did, wanting to return. As an old sage once said, "You can lead a horse to water but you can't make it drink." The instructor's role is to make the horse thirsty.

## Learners' Concerns in the First Class Session: Using the PERC Model

Learners have diverse feelings, thoughts, and questions as they begin a new learning experience. Pratt (1984) has devised a model for dealing with these feelings and questions about a course or workshop: "People need a predictable basis for interacting and will do so whether an instructor guides the process or not. Norms and expectations evolve naturally and inevitably. Yet, when the process is left to chance, problems arise due to ambiguity or misunderstanding. Such problems usually relate to purpose, expectations, roles, or content (PERC) and can be avoided or reduced if these elements are clarified at the outset" (Pratt, 1984, p. 7). In order to clarify these elements, Pratt devised a number of questions that should be raised in connection with the learning experience. He recommends that instructors take time during the first class session to address them. Exhibit 1 is a checklist of questions for instructors, adapted from Pratt's work.

By taking time during the first class session to create a positive and open climate for learning and by addressing the natural feelings and questions adults frequently bring to the classroom, an instructor can go a long way toward establishing an environment that promotes growth for everyone involved. Pratt's PERC model, together with the other suggestions noted earlier, offers a good road map to follow.

## Conclusion

Instruction of adults can be a most gratifying experience, but because of their vast experiential base and potential for high motivation, the challenge of teaching and learning is especially great. At the same time, adults bring numerous feelings, questions, and doubts about a course or workshop that, left unheeded, can dampen the true potential for everyone involved. By anticipating these feelings and thoughts, organizing instructional efforts accordingly, and taking steps during the first class session to promote an effective climate, an instructor can ensure the overall success of the teaching and learning process. As Highet (1950, p. 57) observed more than forty years ago, "Togetherness is the essence of teaching."

## Exhibit 1. Instructor's Questions for the First Class Session

*Directions:* Use the following questions as guides for thinking about the first few hours that you spend with learners. The blank can be checked as you consider each one.

### Purposes

_____ How can you help individual students relate the learning experience to their individual needs?

_____ How can the course help students face personal difficulties at home or work?

_____ How will the course relate to other courses that students may currently have or have already taken?

_____ Why should a student take this particular course?

### Expectations

_____ What should you expect of students in terms of work load and the scheduling of time?

_____ How similar or dissimilar are the students and what are possible consequences of numerous dissimilarities?

_____ What individual problems or situations may exist for which you may need to work out special arrangements?

### Roles

_____ How will you be perceived by various learners?

_____ What kinds of assistance can you give to various learners?

_____ What are your views about learners' disagreements with you in class and how can you communicate such views?

_____ How can you help learners feel at ease with their active planning and participation in learning experiences?

### Content

_____ How can you communicate to learners what they can expect to learn and what they should study?

_____ What can you say about the time required and allowed for practicing and applying course information?

_____ How can you help individual learners feel comfortable about their abilities to compete with other course participants?

## References

Apps, J. W. *Improving Practice in Continuing Education: Modern Approaches for Understanding the Field and Determining Priorities.* San Francisco: Jossey-Bass, 1985.

Apps, J. W. "Foundations for Effective Teaching." In E. R. Hayes (ed.), *Effective Teaching Styles.* New Directions for Adult and Continuing Education, no. 43. San Francisco: Jossey-Bass, 1989.

Brookfield, S. D. *The Skillful Teacher.* San Francisco: Jossey-Bass, 1990.

Draves, W. A. *How to Teach Adults.* Manhattan, Kans.: Learning Resources Network, 1984.

Hiemstra, R., and Sisco, B. *Individualizing Instruction: Making Learning Personal, Empowering, and Successful.* San Francisco: Jossey-Bass, 1990.

Highet, G. *The Art of Teaching.* New York: Knopf, 1950.

Knowles, M. S. *The Modern Practice of Adult Education: From Pedagogy to Andragogy.* (Rev. ed.) New York: Cambridge University Press, 1980.

Knox, A. B. *Helping Adults Learn: A Guide to Planning, Implementing, and Conducting Programs.* San Francisco: Jossey-Bass, 1986.

Pratt, D. D. "Teaching Adults: A Conceptual Framework for the First Session." *Lifelong Learning: An Omnibus of Practice and Research,* 1984, 7 (6), 7–9, 28, 31.

Sisco, B. R. "Adult Learning Processes." In K. E. Plank (ed.), *Mountain States Journeyman and Apprentice Instructor Training Seminar Curriculum Manual.* (2nd ed.) Laramie: University of Wyoming Press, 1987.

*Burton R. Sisco is associate professor of adult education and coordinator of the adult education graduate program at the University of Wyoming, Laramie. Active in professional associations and author of numerous publications, he also is co-editor of the* MPAEA Journal of Adult Education.

*Adults can carry into a learning environment external and internal "baggage" that adversely affects their abilities to engage in learning experiences.*

# Adverse Baggage in the Learning Environment

*V. L. Mike Mahoney*

Adult participation in learning activities can be inhibited for various reasons. Cross (1981) categorizes three types of barriers to learning based on a national survey by the Commission on Non-Traditional Study. Of the three—situational, institutional, and dispositional barriers—the latter ranked relatively low in significance and difficulty. The survey, however, examined reasons for nonparticipation from a primarily scholastic point of view, as indicated by the instruction "Circle *all* those [items listed] that you feel are important in keeping you from learning what you want to learn" (Cross, 1981, p. 99).

As many readers of this volume recognize, reasons for nonparticipation exist below the surface of declared responses. These reasons can be traced to the environmental factors to which adults are exposed at home, at work, and in the community. As extracurricular influences, these factors are in effect "baggage," brought into every learning situation, whether basic education or university graduate study, by their adult "carriers." For the teaching-learning transaction to be most successful, teachers of adults must approach any learning environment with a holistic concern about the everyday problems adults face, some generated by the culture, some by academic conditions, and some by family pressures. This adverse environmental baggage is generally of two types: (1) *external,* reflecting situations in which individuals find themselves at work, at home, or in the community and (2) *internal,* referring to an individual's health, interpersonal conflicts, and attitudes toward a problem or situation.

To illustrate these obstructions, several true vignettes are presented here that typify the kinds of situations faced by teachers who have been

NEW DIRECTIONS FOR ADULT AND CONTINUING EDUCATION, no. 50, Summer 1991 © Jossey-Bass Inc., Publishers challenged to find better ways to facilitate adult learning. In some cases, the eventual resolutions of the problems confronted are reported. In other cases, the resolutions, if any, are not known, but the circumstances reported still highlight the need to consider very carefully what can be done to improve learning environments. Names have been changed in all of the vignettes to protect the privacy of the individuals involved.

## External Baggage

Externally generated baggage can take many different forms and come from at least three sources: family obligations, job duties, and community responsibilities. The first includes the time required or desired for interaction with one's spouse, child rearing, family recreation, and assistance with education of the young. The second pertains to work hours, loyalty to organization, and ethical relationships among employees. The third ranges from helping a neighbor repair a fence, to attending religious services, to serving on a church or service club board. In meeting these responsibilities adult learners are pulled away from learning activity requiring them to seek ways to effectively balance time for learning with time for fulfilling other, extracurricular commitments.

In the following situations the baggage constitutes barriers beyond the individuals' control, given their knowledge and resources. In the first vignette the adult education system in place was inadequate in helping the person overcome the barrier. In the second situation, in contrast, a network of people made it possible for the adult learner to succeed by helping her reduce the load of environmental baggage. Each vignette describes the baggage of the situation and concludes with a description of how the problem was resolved, if at all, and the roles that others played in helping the individual.

> Robert, a building custodian, was working two jobs. His first was as a permanent, full-time maintenance supervisor, the second was running a cleaning service for commercial offices. Both jobs were required to support two children and a sister, who was working in a low-paying job. In his self-employed status Robert worked four hours a day, six days a week. Robert's schedule allowed no time to attend a basic education center in order to prepare for the general equivalency diploma (GED) test. The only help available was from a college teacher who loaned Robert some workbooks on preparing for the exam. Even though he worked in a large city, no learning center was open on Saturday afternoons or Sundays, before 8:00 A.M. and after 9:30 P.M. on weekdays. Robert never attended a GED program because none were available during his free time. It is not known whether he ever received a GED certificate.

Susan was the number-two employee in leadership in a large work unit. Official company policy was to support education and training so that employees could move into higher-level jobs whenever an opportunity was present. For some programs the company reimbursed tuition and book expenses. Although the work unit supervisor outwardly supported the policy for all subordinates, he treated Susan differently. Each term, when Susan applied for company educational assistance, her after-hours work load suddenly increased. Susan soon realized the supervisor was assigning her late rush work only on class days, thus causing her to miss or be late for class. The subliminal message from the supervisor was clear: "Don't challenge me!" After complaining about this interference several times, but not seeing corrective action being taken, Susan attacked the problem in a different way. She discussed it with an instructor and some other students who suggested that she wait until the term was well along before applying for educational assistance. By not voluntarily sharing class schedules with the supervisor, Susan protected herself and was able to attend every class the next term.

The first vignette illustrates the predicament of an energetic building custodian who sought a better way of life but had no apparent services available to meet his needs. Susan's scenario demonstrates resourcefulness in handling the baggage manufactured by a defensive supervisor. Most of us have no doubt encountered similar or other scenarios where external baggage in some way hampered an adult's efforts to learn.

## Internal Baggage

Internally generated baggage can be an even greater burden. This burden may stem from an unwillingness to deal with a problem, from not recognizing a need, from a desire for privacy to protect oneself against discrimination, or from an inner commitment to self and family. In each of the following vignettes the environmental baggage is very personal. In one instance learning to read was not a high priority until misfortune happened. Health problems faced by another family member are a factor in the other situation, which could have led to personal health problems for the adult learner had she continued to drive herself too hard. In each instance, the issues were resolved through the efforts of a teacher or network of people who helped create a better learning environment.

Joe, a forty-five-year-old carpenter, lived in a semirural community. Family economic difficulties forced Joe to drop out of school in the second grade. With hard work, he had developed a reputation as a skilled carpenter and was in high demand to remodel homes and make fine cabinets. People admired his skill of quickly making numerical calculations, especially in his head. One day, though, when preparing an estimate on a prospective remodeling job, his pick-up truck, parked on a neighboring lot, disappeared. When Joe learned his truck was gone, he called the police, who told him that he had parked it illegally, all because he could not read the "Tow Away Zone" sign. That was when Joe began a reading program, determined to learn to read as quickly as possible. For many years Joe had been a "rock hound," and he and a close friend had collected dozens of excellent mineral specimens. All were mounted and properly identified on a beautiful display board that Joe's friend had labeled with both common and scientific names. Joe had memorized the names and properties of each mineral. His reading teacher capitalized on Joe's great interest in mineralogy by using learning materials specifically oriented to the sciences. In only five months Joe advanced several grade levels in his reading skills.

Christina was a thirty-eight-year-old Hispanic doctoral student from south Texas. She was the first of several children in the family to enter graduate school and the first to pursue a doctorate. For four successive terms she commuted eight hundred miles every weekend, determined to finish a doctorate before her father died of a terminal illness. The financial drain as well as her commitment to pursuing the degree weighed heavily on Christina. Her dedication quickly became evident to faculty and students alike. As faculty learned of her need to complete the degree work within a short but realistic time frame, informal counseling was provided to reassure and encourage her. Other adjustments were made so that she could meet unscheduled, weekend family obligations. After three and a half years, Christina received the degree, while her mother and father (then in very poor health) and many other family members from towns hundreds of miles away witnessed the event.

These stories describe two more adult learners and the internal baggage controlling each. In the first, Joe was shocked into learning to read when his truck was taken, and a teacher subsequently capitalized on Joe's interest in science. Christina carried the baggage of family honor and poor health of her father, but she was still determined to demonstrate that she could compete successfully in a different culture, especially when others began helping her cope with the situation.

## Thermometer for Measuring Personal Baggage

Can internal and external environmental baggage, such as that described in the above vignettes, be measured in terms of potential interference with teaching and learning transactions? Can a teacher of adults discern the implications of any baggage? Obviously, some baggage is more of a burden than is other baggage. Thus in-depth examination of the impact of various constraints on adult learning would be quite useful to the concerns addressed here.

The Social Readjustment Rating Scale (Holmes and Rahe, 1967) has potential for measuring personal baggage. It was developed to assess the impact of various external stressors, based on assigned values (for example, 100 points maximum for death of a spouse), on a person's well-being. The list of stressor events constitutes a reference scale for checking off those events in a person's life that have occurred in the preceding six to twelve months. Total point values of the checked items indicate the probability level that stress-related illness will occur during the following year: the higher the total points, the greater the probability.

The Social Readjustment Rating Scale does not explicitly take into account age or cultural differences. It also does not account for temporal factors such as death of a spouse after one year of marriage versus after twenty years, or for areas of everyday experience that are difficult to quantify such as the level of marital satisfaction. Furthermore, it does not necessarily take into account the diversity of social norms that exists across culturally and economically distinct types of communities. Nonetheless, the scale identifies more than forty factors and life events that can affect the efforts of people pursuing learning activities. In short, the scale provides an initial point for considering the impact of various factors on adults' readiness to learn.

Based on the Social Readjustment Rating Scale, I have developed a "thermometer" or guide for evaluating the impact of various internal and external life events on an individual's ability to engage in the learning process (see Table 1). The thermometer is not a rating scale, however. Rather, the "temperature values" are useful in accounting for the varying degrees of impact that events can have on participation in adult education programs. Just as a person's body temperature can vary from morning to night, so too can the thermometer's factors exert greater or lesser impact on the adult learner within relatively short time frames.

For example, a forced relocation to a new city because the husband was transferred typically produces immediate trauma (external baggage) for the husband, wife, and children. For the husband, though, an immediate immersion in the job usually results in new friends, increasing feelings of value to the organization, and growing knowledge of the community. However, the wife and children may take many months before appropriate adjustments (often internal baggage in nature) are made. Consequently, for one person the move may be a burden for many weeks or months, thus interfering with learning efforts. But for another person it may generate only limited interference with work or learning.

Table 1 lists thirty-seven events (including the marital separation categories) that can adversely affect the learning process. This is only a prelimi-

## Table 1. "Temperature" Changes Due to Significant Life Events, by Time Interval Since Event Occurrence

| | Degree Rise in "Temperature" | | |
|---|---|---|---|
| Event | 0–3 Months | 3–6 Months | 6–12 Months |
| Death of spouse: married 20+ years | 5 | 4 | 5 |
| Death of spouse: married 0–1 year | 5 | 4 | 3 |
| Death of an adult child | 6 | 5 | 4 |
| Death of an infant child | 4 | 4 | 3 |
| Death of a parent | 4 | 3 | 2 |
| Lawsuit: custody or guardianship | 4 | 4 | 4 |
| Divorce: married more than 20 years[a] | 4 | 4 | 4 |
| Divorce: married 10–20 years[a] | 4 | 4 | 3 |
| Divorce: married less than 2 years[a] | 4 | 3 | 2 |
| Job lost: company merger | 4 | 3 | 3 |
| Out of work | 3 | 4 | 5 |
| Out of work: accident | 3 | 3 | 3 |
| Terminal illness: self or spouse | 5 | 4 | 4 |
| Terminal illness: family member | 4 | 4 | 4 |
| Loss of family home | 5 | 4 | 4 |
| Substance abuse in family | 5 | 4 | 4 |
| Denied promotion or job reassigned | 5 | 4 | 3 |
| Personal conflict: between spouses | 4 | 3 | 2 |
| Personal conflict: with neighbors | 3 | 1 | 1 |
| Personal conflict: with co-worker(s) | 3 | 1 | 1 |
| Loss of one-third or more of family income | 4 | 3 | 2 |
| New job: good match to qualifications | 2 | 2 | 1 |
| New job: underemployed for qualifications | 3 | 3 | 2 |
| Death of close friend | 2 | 1 | 0 |
| Pregnancy: unwanted and unexpected | 5 | 4 | 2 |
| Pregnancy: delayed and desired | 4 | 2 | 2 |
| Family member sent into military combat | 4 | 3 | 3 |
| Lawsuit as plaintiff or defendant | 5 | 3 | 1 |
| Loss of family/personal friendships | 3 | 1 | 0 |
| Recognition for personal achievement | 1 | 0 | 0 |
| Forced relocation to a new city | 4 | 3 | 1 |
| Work schedule change not acceptable | 3 | 2 | 1 |
| Child severely disciplined at school | 2 | 1 | 0 |
| Child charged with felony crime | 4 | 2 | 2 |

[a] For marital separation, deduct 2 degrees from the divorce scores, per each category.

nary effort to develop a measuring device. Clearly, additional research is needed to refine and validate the event categories and values of impact. For example, the events are not exhaustive; many more can be added. The suggested values are based primarily on personal observations of how most of these events have, at one time or another, affected adult learning commitments and interest over the time periods shown. The table also identifies events that cause people to turn to a learning activity ("loss of job") and those that hamper a learning effort.

The "temperature" values should be thought of as indices of the amount of interference a learner may experience at stated time periods after an event. Extending the thermometer metaphor and using body temperature as a reference point, addition of the suggested values shown in the table to a baseline 98.6 degrees for a given event can help a teacher understand how that event affects the learner at that moment. In addition, the teacher can examine the nature of the interference in order to devise strategies to minimize the event's impact on learning, that is, to "lower" the temperature.

Using the figures in the table, for example, it is suggested that the death of an adult child raises one's temperature 6 degrees in the first three months. The resulting temperature of 104.6 degrees indicates that the learner is under considerable stress, which is likely to interfere with any learning activity. If the learning effort is channeled toward resolution of stress, such as a death and illness support group, the learner might experience at least some relief. Directed toward other purposes (such as job training), the effort may accomplish little. In evaluation of the impact of an event, a person's age, gender, and cultural background can be highly significant in terms of the amount of temperature increase resulting from the event.

## Constraints on Learning and Teacher Assistance

If a teacher of adults can identify some of the internal and external baggage or some of the "temperature" changes due to significant life events that have potential for affecting learners, what can then be done? As illustrations of both internal and external baggage, this section describes six common constraints with which adult learners must contend. Several actions that a teacher can take in identifying these constraints and helping learners to make adjustments are briefly detailed to suggest some of the possibilities for problem resolution.

**Family Responsibilities.** These constraints stem from a self-imposed commitment to family. Their significance in terms of impact depends on an adult learner's economic level, educational or financial level, and associated cultural or ethnic background. For some adults the experience of taking children to the mall, the movies, or the park may be very important in maintaining family life. For others, the activities of supporting the family through Little League coaching or baking cakes or making chili for church suppers may be the best way of preserving family connections and building strong family ties.

When a teacher acknowledges and shows respect for these activities, adult learners build a corresponding respect for learning activities and assignments. The process of getting to know adult learners in an informal way, such as by hosting a potluck supper for class members, offers countless benefits to the teacher in the form of increased understanding of each learner's culture, needs, and interests.

**Job Requirements.** Job requirements and expectations also can constrain an adult's learning effort. Company owners and managers may emphasize the importance of education or training so that their companies can compete successfully in the marketplace. But this support often translates into "You better get with it, because you may not have a job if the company goes under." The learner then may perceive various kinds of pressures. "If I don't keep up, I may lose my job." "Others are eager and pushing me from below." "I resent having to give up my personal time when I should be with my family."

By being alert to job-related constraints, the teacher can better understand learners' attitudes toward learning, their desire to leapfrog basic material, or their impatience with learning. To create a more positive attitude, the teacher should select and use material that helps a learner better understand the work environment in terms of economic problems, a company's ability to compete in the marketplace, or changing knowledge requirements associated with constantly changing technology. This approach enables the learner to share at work what has been gained in class, often generating increased respect from the employer who will see direct benefits from company-sponsored education.

**Community Commitments.** A third external source of constraints relates to a variety of community-based obligations, such as church commitments, associations with neighborhood groups, and membership in service clubs. Taken together these constraints are particularly problematic because the community groups involved support many worthwhile projects and reflect interests in family and society to which an adult has committed skills, talents, and time. Thus, the learner often must adjust personal schedules in order to benefit fully from a learning activity, which generates a sense of loss for learners who see themselves as separated from active participation in community life.

To offset feelings of loss such as these, the teacher can identify or develop learning materials related to programs that various interest groups support. Some learning experiences could involve visits to or study of community agencies. To help learners further develop writing, speaking, or presentational skills, they can be asked to describe information about the community programs or activities in which they have participated.

**Self-Expectations.** Adults also often have internal or personal constraints that affect their learning efforts. For example, self-expectations sometimes have little to do with what is required in a learning activity. For some learners there are self-expectations of unnecessarily high performance; for others there is dissatisfaction with not receiving the highest possible grade on an assignment. Another discouraging self-expectation is the notion that "I've been away from school too long and there is no way I can keep up with younger people."

Through informal one-to-one talks and careful observations during group and class activities, teachers can identify such adverse baggage or constraints. One way to help such students is to point to others' success, saying, "If they can do it, so can you!" Another way is to use pretests and posttests of subject matter, skills, or concepts such as are commonly found in diagnostic tests for basic education, English as a second language, and high school equivalency programs. Such testing can provide reinforcement to perfectionists and can reassure those learners who may doubt their learning abilities.

**Health Problems.** Everyone is susceptible to different types of health problems during adult life, and certain illnesses or disabilities are commonly associated with specific stages of human development. A broken bone may be discomforting and a nuisance for a young adult but can be a major handicap for a senior citizen.

The teacher needs to be alert to health-related constraints and the stresses they may impose on the learner. Some learners can be counseled to join support groups. Extra time and help can be given to assist any learner with a particular disability in coping with learning requirements. In some instances, a particular health problem can even have curriculum-building potential, such as teaching about coping skills or the new learning acquired through study of a disease or illness.

**Feelings of Self-Worth.** At one time or other, every person hears that he or she "should" do such and such. We grow up hearing these words, and as long as parents are around we will continue to hear "You ought to do that!" These judgments also surface in adult life, for example, when an adult student tells the company bowling team that the course schedule precludes bowling on Thursday nights and the response comes forth that "you're letting down the team." This type of constraint also is part of the environmental baggage, the human part buried deep in our psyches that we bring to the learning situation. Spoken or limited, various messages come through from well-meaning friends, relatives, and others that affect our feelings of self-worth.

Such challenges to adults who want to pursue their learning activities require special attention and consideration from teachers if the barriers are to be overcome. Sensitivity, inventiveness, and creativity are needed if teachers are to help learners attain their goals. Teachers often must provide positive reinforcement, facilitating learners by working with them in small groups on various activities while they build up confidence and learning skills.

## Conclusion

Educators of adults have many opportunities and options to enhance the learning experience and help learners overcome constraints generated by various environmental factors. The externally generated and the internally generated baggage discussed here involves only limited aspects of the relevant issues. To these can be added circadian rhythm (Brown, Hastings, and Palmer, 1970), the mechanism that dictates when we are at our best time of day or night to engage in different tasks, an area little explored relative to its impact on adult learning. Cranton (1989), while taking into account learning styles and ways to manipulate the environment to enhance adult learning, cites ways to match methods to domain and level of learning. The influence of the personal environment of the learner needs to be further addressed in that context.

## References

Brown, F. A., Jr., Hastings, J. W., and Palmer, J. D. *The Biological Clock: Two Views.* Orlando, Fla.: Academic Press, 1970.

Cranton, P. *Planning Instruction for Adult Learners.* Toronto: Wall & Thompson, 1989.

Cross, K. P. *Adults as Learners: Increasing Participation and Facilitating Learning.* San Francisco: Jossey-Bass, 1981.

Holmes, T. H., and Rahe, R. H. "The Social Readjustment Rating Scale." *Journal of Psychosomatic Research,* 1967, *11,* 213–218.

*V. L. Mike Mahoney is associate professor in the Department of Secondary and Higher Education at East Texas State University, Commerce. He coordinates the graduate program in adult and continuing education at the university and researches and teaches about environmental issues in adult education.*

*"The problem of the twentieth century is the problem of color-line"*
*(Dubois, 1969, p. 36).*

# Perceptual Patterns and the Learning Environment: Confronting White Racism

*Scipio A. J. Colin III, Trudie Kibbe Preciphs*

As adult educators develop greater tools and resources for dealing with a multiracial society and world, we are challenged to enlarge our understanding of the influence of racism on perceptual patterns and the teaching-learning process. Therefore, an understanding of the role and importance of perceptual patterns must become an integral part of the educational process. This chapter focuses on the development of individual perceptual patterns and provides insights about how racism is reflected in adult education practice. Finally, potential solutions to the problem of racism in the educational system are offered, each designed to enhance learning experiences.

Racism is a social problem that adversely affects learning environments. As Hogan (1969, p. 148) asserts, "It is imperative that we [educators] examine critically the influence of racism and social class bias on educational personnel, the promulgation of racism through the theory and the attitudes of school personnel." As the field of adult education moves into the twenty-first century, it is imperative to acknowledge that this current period in American history continues to exemplify the historical contradiction between espoused democratic ideals and the separate racial societies that were created by law and are now maintained by tradition. The assumptions and implications of Social Darwinism, the eugenics movement, and the Teutonic origins theory are the intellectual antecedents of the sociocultural racism that exists today. Disturbingly, these assumptions of racial superiority and inferiority still influence our perceptual, attitudinal, and behavioral patterns (Berkhofer, 1978; Gosset, 1963; Jordan, 1968; Stanton, 1960).

If the field of adult education is to meet the needs of all adult learners, practitioners must acknowledge the existence and ramifications of racism and understand its overall impact on their perceptions. For example, perceptions are capable of influencing beliefs, attitudes, and behavior that, in turn, affect teacher-learner interactions.

It is difficult to offer a single definition of racism since the ideology is illogical in principle and diverse in practice. Many social researchers have concluded that the exclusion and subordination of nonwhite groups is based on color (Delaney, 1970; Ehrlich and Feldman, 1977; Fredrickson, 1971; Kovel, 1971; Sealacek and Brooks, 1976; Welsing, 1972). But the most widely used and accepted definition is provided by the U.S. Commission on Civil Rights (1970, p. 5): "Racism may be viewed as an attitude, action, or institutional structure which subordinates a person or group because of color . . . it is the visibility of skin color—and of other physical traits associated with particular colors or groups—that marks individuals as 'targets' for subordination by members of the white majority. Specifically, white racism subordinates members of all groups primarily because they are not white in color."

Given this definition, it would seem that white Americans are racist as a result of the connotative meaning that is given to their skin color. Adult education practitioners may be discomforted by the use of the descriptor "white racism," but it is our contention that (1) racism permeates the roots of American society and is reflected in all its societal institutions, and that (2) racism was created by white Americans and is perpetuated by them. Racism may be conscious or subconscious and is expressed in actions or attitudes initiated by individuals, groups, or institutions that treat human beings unjustly because of their skin pigmentation. Therefore, racism is reflected in attitudes, behavior, and institutions.

Adult educators must clearly understand the power and privilege of skin pigmentation in American society. Past research has shown that it is indeed color that determines the quality and quantity of interaction between educational practitioners who are members of the dominant racial group and learners from nonwhite racial groups (Rosenthal, 1973; Rosenthal and Jacobsen, 1968; Rubovitz and Maehr, 1973). Almost nowhere in adult education literature and research is racism recognized as an integral and influential part of American life that requires our immediate attention. Instead, the field has chosen to focus on the non-threatening manifestations of racism, such as low socioeconomic status (SES), motivation, and participation. We believe that as a result of this avoidance behavior, many adult educators are totally unaware of the extent to which theories and research reflect and reinforce white racist attitudes and assumptions about the purported inferiority of nonwhite learners. This behavior influences adult education practice and sustains perceptions that impede learning.

## Perceptual Patterns

Perceptual patterns are consistent views of the world based on mental images formulated from the standards and ideals of the individual's social reference group. Perceptual patterns are reinforced through images, attitudes, and behavior.

Recently, the influence of racism on the development of perceptual, attitudinal, and behavioral patterns of nonwhite adult learners has been analyzed and discussed within the theoretical framework of self-ethnic reflectors (Colin, 1988, 1989). What have yet to be discussed are the impact of racism on the development of practitioners' perceptual patterns and how these patterns impede the teaching-learning process.

Racism is rooted in dysfunctional belief systems resulting from distorted perceptions formed over a period of time. We cannot ignore the significant role of the sociocultural environment in shaping perceptual patterns. According to Doobs (1947, p. 138), attitudes are a "readiness or proclivity of an individual to respond in a certain way toward something." This response readiness is the result of overt and covert learning that eventually becomes automatic. Blair, Jones, and Simpson (1963, p. 217) state that attitudes endure because "they operate in perception. . . . [People] tend to see what [they are] looking for and hence will find reinforcement for already existing attitudes even though there is evidence to the contrary." This tendency illustrates how perceptions are formed into patterns and then perpetuated. One can surmise that the image construct is a major factor in the development of perceptual patterns. Image construction is visual; what one sees initially with the "mind's eye" forms attitudes that are based on assumptions regarding racial superiority and inferiority. These attitudes in turn govern or dictate behavior.

Wolpe's (1973) research has shown that habits are not perceived by the individual as either good or bad. Therefore, the images that whites have of nonwhite racial groups have been so ingrained that questions of validity simply do not arise. Such is the habitual nature of the visualization process. When there is continued reinforcement through miseducation, the negative perceptual process is strengthened. This reinforcement triad of images, attitudes, and behavior affects both the personal and professional lives of practitioners. These perceptual patterns are reflected in the attitudinal and behavioral "baggage" that the white practitioner brings into the learning environment. For example, upon seeing nonwhite students, the internal connotative meanings given to color are triggered. As stated by Blair, Jones, and Simpson (1963, p. 227), "Attitudes are wrapped up with a person's feelings, needs, and self-concept. To let them go requires a change in self. Furthermore, attitudes are easy to maintain because [persons] see what [they] want to see and may distort reality so as to find evidence to support any position [they] want to hold."

Because practitioners tend to hold onto negative perceptions, white racism is perpetuated. Consequently, distorted perceptions lead to what we refer to as "perceptual deprivation," or the inability of individuals to observe experience, actions, and behavior without biased interpretation. Illustrations of perceptual deprivation are as follows.

*Writing Skills and Standards.* A white practitioner encounters a Hispanic student who is in fact a third-generation American citizen. When the learner's writing does not meet "the standard," the practitioner assumes, as an explanation, that English is the student's second language, rather than realizing that the learner simply has not mastered good writing skills.

*Perceptions of Self-Ethnic Image.* When an African-American student is encountered, the practitioner assumes that the learner has a low self-ethnic image and lacks motivation, both of which are major obstacles to learning. The perception produces certain assumptions regarding the abilities and capabilities of the learner. Therefore, if the work of learners does not meet "the standard," the assumption is that substandard work is the best they can do. In turn, this assumption influences the quantity and quality of teacher-learner interaction.

The influence of culture on individuals is significant in the learning process. Lovell (1986, p. 88) asserts that "all changes in an individual's social behavior involve learning. The process by which . . . [individuals] come to accept attitudes, values, and norms of the social group of which . . . [they are] members is referred to as socialization." Because it is the dominant racial group's culture that is transmitted through the socialization process, the result is "perceptual deprivation." The two major socializing factors within American society are education and the media.

**Education and the Media.** All adult education practitioners have one characteristic in common—the ethnocentric content of their prior education experience. For white Americans, the curricular content has always reflected their sociocultural and intellectual histories and their worldview. Thus, they have been socialized to see themselves in a positive-primary mode, and nonwhite racial groups in a negative-secondary mode. These perceptions are neither challenged nor contradicted by the media. The term *media* here refers to television, print, and motion pictures (Lapides and Burrows, 1971; Randall, 1980).

An illustration of how the media reinforce distorted perceptions involves the publication of the revised edition of *Great Books of the Western World.* The exclusion of the intellectual works of African-Americans has created a controversy (McCalope, 1990). In explaining this exclusion, the editor-in-chief, Mortimer Adler, stated the following: "I think probably in the next century there will be some Black that writes a great book, but there hasn't been so far" (McCalope, 1990, p. 14). In reply, Henry Lewis Gates, Jr., an African-American historian, stated, "Intellectually, we are still represented in this society as not being smart enough and that is just an undeniable remnant of racism" (McCalope, 1990, p. 14). Racism is further reinforced through motion pictures and television, which portray African-Americans as athletes and entertainers rather than as scholars.

**Labeling.** Another form of socialization comes about through labeling. According to Colin (1987, 1988), the connotative meanings of low SES are "disadvantaged," "culturally deprived," "dropouts," and "minorities." Such language reinforces the distorted perceptions of nonwhite learners. SES is used in the literature to explain the lack of motivation, the minimal or total absence of participation in education, and the peripheral position of non-whites in America. The SES label only serves to describe where these groups are in the social hierarchy in regard to status. Why they are there is not really considered outside of the standard explanations of poverty, cultural depravity, and inferior education. Yet, to glibly dismiss race as possibly the major determinator of educational attainment, occupational status, and income is to take a dangerous leap of faith. Sociologists and historians are still deeply divided over whether race or class is more important in terms of influencing SES. Adult educators must be wary as well in assuming that "class" is more important.

Mislabeling basically serves two purposes: (1) It provides researchers with a rationale for not focusing on race as an impact factor. And (2) it places responsibility and blame for failure on the learner. Studies that have examined the influence of race on SES have clearly shown that there is a direct correlation between race and educational attainment, occupation, and income. Even when there is no discrepancy relative to the amount of formal education between whites and nonwhites, there is still a significant gap in income (Alba and Moore, 1982; Colin, 1987; Ogbu, 1978; "Report Defines Three Levels of Black Life," 1990).

**Role of Adult Education.** Adult education philosophies, purposes, goals, and programs generally have been developed by white Americans for white Americans, and that white Americans have not relinquished or shared this power, raises two questions: In what way does the field reflect and reinforce negative perceptions of nonwhite adult learners held by practitioners? How does the practitioners' perceptions of nonwhite learners impede the learning process?

In addressing the first question we need to examine the content of graduate programs. In courses focusing on the historical development of adult education, both intellectual and institutional, nonwhite racial groups in the United States are rarely mentioned as the creators of concepts or ideas, or as producers of curricula. Typically, they are only mentioned in courses with such titles as "Teaching the Disadvantaged Adult" or "Teaching Strategies for Special Populations," or in courses dealing with participation research. On the basis of these experiences, learners reach one of two conclusions: (1) These groups made no contribution, which suggests intellectual inferiority and deficiencies, or (2) there is a conscious exclusion of their involvement. Adult education, by it nature and design, is ethnocentric, and nonwhite involvement simply does not meet the dominant racial group's standard (Colin, 1988).

**Teaching-Learning Transaction.** The teaching-learning transaction is a basic component of an effective learning environment. This component can be measured by the degree of interaction between practitioner and learner. Park and Burgess (1924) stated that one manifestation of racism is the social distance that dominant racial group members put between themselves and other racial groups.

A result of perceptual deprivation is that social distance adversely affects the quantity and quality of the interaction between the practitioner and nonwhite learners. The distance is reflected in either a lack of interaction or a negative interaction. We cannot ignore the implications of Sowell's (1972) observation that the perceptions held by white educators about nonwhite learners are the source of the problem, not the learners.

## Recommendations

Because perceptual deprivation is best addressed and confronted in the learning environment, adult educators should assume a functional role in eradicating distorted perceptions that foster cultural oppression and racism. For example, in a case study of adult volunteers, the findings supported dramatic change in the belief systems of a majority of the study population after efforts to eradicate distorted perceptions (Preciphs, 1989). Such changes occurred as a result of both informal and formal learning experiences that focused on racism and other social issues. Formal learning experiences consisted of structured events such as workshops, presentations, oral histories, and explications of traditions through storytelling, sensitivity groups, and focused group sessions. Informal learning experiences were unstructured, wherein unexpected and unanticipated learning was facilitated by peer dialogue relative to prior structured events. The key study components identified as responsible for changing perceptions were (1) acknowledgment by adult education practitioners that racism exists, (2) commitment by adult education practitioners to address racism in the learning environment, (3) exchange of information about other cultures and life experiences, (4) utilization of the affective domain of learning to facilitate critical self-reflection, and (5) assessment of learning experiences.

Because the aforementioned five components have been shown to facilitate the kind of critical self-reflection necessary for change in perceptions and beliefs, they are recommended bases for confronting white racism in adult education learning environments:

*Stage One: Acknowledgment of Racism.* First, the task of confronting perceptual deprivation in learning environments requires that practitioners acknowledge the existence of racism. Second, white practitioners must then understand the role that they play in perpetuating racism. Implicit in this acknowledgment is the significant part adult educators can play in confronting distorted perceptual patterns that foster not only racism but also other forms of harmful "isms." Likewise, acknowledgment of personal racism promotes greater sensitivity with regard to course planning, program development, research, and classroom facilitation. Failure to acknowledge racism serves to perpetuate it in learning environments and in society at large.

*Stage Two: Commitment to Address Racism in the Learning Environment.* Following acknowledgment of racism, it is essential that practitioners utilize the learning environment to actively address and confront racism. While racism may be the focus of a particular seminar, ongoing attention to this problem is necessary. Both white and nonwhite practitioners may assume a role in sharing personal histories as a part of the course content. Key to this stage is the importance of practitioners' examination of personal perceptions and roles related to dominant racial group behavior. Furthermore, practitioners must become more conscious of the subtle and direct forms of racism that they are capable of transmitting to learners. Nonverbal behavior is one form of subtle racism that is conveyed by social distance and trivialization of issues. Only by confronting individual racism can practitioners enhance the learning process.

*Stage Three: Exchange of Information About Other Cultures and Histories.* It is vital that the curricula within adult education adequately reflect the cultures and histories of nonwhite groups. The importance of this stage rests in its potential to confront perceptual patterns that have been distorted due to inadequate information about nonwhite groups. Therefore, appreciation for other cultures and histories is a necessary precondition for confronting racism in the learning environment.

*Stage Four: Utilization of the Affective Domain of Learning.* This stage tends to be the most painful for practitioners, for here they recognize the ramifications of their dominant racial group behavior. Perceptual deprivation can be confronted and even eradicated by exposing adults to significant emotional experiences within learning environments (Preciphs, 1989). Such experiences are for purposes of learning rather than for manipulation, indoctrination, or establishment of guilt. Significant emotional experiences, in the context of the learning environment, serve to subconsciously trigger a connection between painful aspects of individual life experiences and the controversial issue at hand. Specifically, significant emotional experiences, conveyed through oral histories and traditions (storytelling) and shared life experiences, enable learners to relive painful experiences within their own lives. This recollection, in turn, elicits greater empathy for another person's pain and discomfort, thereby creating openness and critical self-reflection. A necessary component of critical self-reflection is the ability to recognize that one's humanity is linked to or holds much in common with the lived experiences of others, regardless of their race or background (Preciphs, 1989).

For learning in this domain to be effective, dialogue is required to enable individuals to get in touch with their feelings and to share these feelings with others. Furthermore, while dialogue is necessary to foster reflection, additional insights may occur from hearing the perspectives of others. Because of the emotional nature of the learning experience, practitioners may want to maintain journals and share new insights with peers.

*Stage Five: Assessment of Learning Experiences.* It is very difficult to assess the impact of learning that occurs within the affective domain. New insights may occur gradually for some individuals and more dramatically for others. While the aim is to eradicate distorted perceptions, the primary success of this learning is based on sensitizing individuals to how perceptions are formed and become distorted.

Practitioners' attention to white racism requires continuous attention. Exhibit 1 provides a checklist that practitioners can use to help them think about and confront issues of racism and to counter perceptual deprivation.

## Conclusion

Adult educators have been consumers of distorted information. As a result, they encounter difficulties in perceiving nonwhite learners as people with unlimited cognitive abilities. As stated by Preciphs (1990), "Adult education can no longer debate whether or not to address social change. To do so

### Exhibit 1. Checklist for Countering the Effects of Perceptual Deprivation

_____ 1. The curriculum, assigned literature, and course content reflect different racial groups.

_____ 2. The contributions and perspectives of nonwhite learners are invited, respected, and valued.

_____ 3. The issues of white racism receive primary attention in the learning environment.

_____ 4. The adult education practitioner communicates the importance of addressing racism as a part of the educational process.

_____ 5. Practitioners are enabled to better understand how negative perceptual patterns foster biases about other racial groups.

_____ 6. Research projects include nonwhite sociocultural histories, orientations, and interpretations.

_____ 7. Learning experiences about racism are ongoing and not confined to a few comments.

_____ 8. Practitioners are becoming more aware of the subtle forms of racism that they perpetuate through their interaction, instructional strategies, and methodologies.

_____ 9. Practitioners exhibit sensitivity toward and awareness of other cultures.

_____ 10. Practitioners become sensitized about the pain and hurt experienced by nonwhite learners who must function within a racist society.

represents a debate of luxury because for many, education for social change is a requirement for survival. Furthermore, the debate is elitist, as it responds to a first-world mentality which is void of a global perspective." Basically, such a debate is a form of perceptual deprivation based on color, power, and geography. As white practitioners address racism in America, the additional challenge is to confront global racism as well.

# References

Alba, R. D., and Moore, G. "Ethnicity in the American Elite." *American Sociological Review,* 1982, *47,* 373–383.
Berkhofer, R. F. *The White Man's Indian: Images of the American Indian from Columbus to the Present.* New York: Knopf, 1978.
Blair, G. M., Jones, R. S., and Simpson, R. H. *Educational Psychology.* New York: Macmillan, 1963.
Colin, S.A.J., III. "SES: The 'Humpty-Dumpty' Method of Labeling." Unpublished manuscript, Graduate Studies in Adult Continuing Education, Northern Illinois University, 1987.
Colin, S.A.J., III. "Voices from Beyond the Veil: Marcus Garvey, the Universal Negro Improvement Association, and the Education of African Ameripean Adults." Unpublished doctoral dissertation, Northern Illinois University, 1988.
Colin, S.A.J., III. "Cultural Literacy: Ethnocentrism Versus Selfethnic Reflectors." *Thresholds in Education,* 1989, *15* (4), 16–19.
Delaney, L. T. "The White American Psyche—Exploration of Racism." In B. Schwartz and R. Disch (eds.), *White Racism: Its History, Pathology, and Practice.* New York: Dell, 1970.
Doobs, L. W. "The Behavior of Attitudes." *Psychological Review,* 1947, *54,* 135–156.
DuBois, W.E.B. *The Souls of Black Folk.* New York: New American Library, 1969. (Originally published in 1903.)
Ehrlich, P. R., and Feldman, S. S. *The Race Bomb: Skin Color, Prejudice, and Intelligence.* New York: Ballantine, 1977.
Fredrickson, G. M. *The Black Image in the White Mind: The Debate on Afro-American Character and Destiny, 1817–1914.* New York: Harper & Row, 1971.
Gosset, T. F. *Race: The History of an Idea in America.* Dallas, Tex.: Southern Methodist University Press, 1963.
Hogan, E. O. "Racism in Educators: A Barrier to Quality Education." In R. L. Green (ed.), *Racial Crisis in American Education.* Chicago: Follett Educational Corporation, 1969.
Jordan, W. *White Over Black: American Attitudes Toward the Negro, 1550–1812.* Chapel Hill: University of North Carolina Press, 1968.
Kovel, J. *White Racism: A Psychohistory.* New York: Vintage, 1971.
Lapides, F. R., and Burrows, D. (eds.). *Racism: A Casebook.* New York: Crowell, 1971.
Lovell, R. B. *Adult Learning.* London, England: Croom-Helm, 1986.
McCalope, M. "Blacks Furious Over Exclusion from *Great Books of the Western World." Jet,* Nov. 17, 1990, pp. 14–18.
Ogbu, J. *Minority Education and Caste: The American System in Cross-Cultural Perspective.* Orlando, Fla.: Academic Press, 1978.
Park, R. E., and Burgess, E. W. *Introduction to the Science of Sociology.* Chicago: University of Chicago Press, 1924.

Preciphs, T. K. "Understanding Adult Learning for Social Action in a Volunteer Setting." Unpublished doctoral dissertation, Teachers College, Columbia University, 1989.

Preciphs, T. K. "The Legacy of Myles Horton: Education for Social Change—The Past as Prologue." Paper presented at the annual meeting of the American Association for Adult and Continuing Education, Salt Lake City, Utah, November 1, 1990.

Randall, M. M. (ed.). The Kaleidoscopic Lens: How Hollywood Views Ethnic Groups. Englewood, N.J.: Ozer, 1980.

"Report Defines Three Levels of Black Life." Jet, July 2, 1990, p. 9.

Rosenthal, R. "The Pygmalion Effect Lives." Psychology Today, 1973, 7, 56–63.

Rosenthal, R., and Jacobsen, L. Pygmalion in the Classroom. New York: Holt, Rinehart & Winston, 1968.

Rubovitz, P., and Maehr, M. L. "Pygmalion Black and White." Journal of Personality and Social Psychology, 1973, 25, 210–218.

Sealacek, W. E., and Brooks, G. C., Jr. Racism in American Revolution: A Model For Change. Chicago: Nelson-Hall, 1976.

Sowell, T. Black Education: Myths and Tragedies. New York: McKay, 1972.

Stanton, W. The Leopard's Spots: Scientific Attitudes Toward Racism in America, 1815–1859. Chicago: University of Chicago Press, 1960.

U.S. Commission on Civil Rights. Racism in America. Clearinghouse Publication Urban Series No. 1. Washington, D.C.: Government Printing Office, 1970.

Welsing, F.L.C. The Cress Theory of Color-Confrontation and Racism (White Supremacy). Washington, D.C.: Frances L. Cress-Welsing, 1972.

Wolpe, J. "Psycho-Therapy by Reciprocal Inhabitation." In C. H. Patterson (ed.), Theories of Counseling and Psycho-Therapy. New York: Harper & Row, 1973.

*Scipio A. J. Colin III is assistant professor of adult and continuing education at North Carolina State University, Raleigh.*

*Trudie Kibbe Preciphs is an adult education practitioner working with volunteers in the United Methodist Church. She is adjunct faculty member at United Theological Seminary in Dayton, Ohio.*

*Institutional settings both create and mirror a learning*
*environment that devalues and disempowers women learners.*

# Women's Trouble: Women, Gender, and the Learning Environment

*Susan Collard, Joyce Stalker*

Primarily in the past decade adult educators have considered the significance of gender to learning and education. The shifts in thinking that have
occurred around this issue are in part due to the increased number (however minimal proportionately) of analyses of gender as related to both the
practice and the study of adult education—for example, Hayes and Smith
(1990), Hughes and Kennedy (1980), Hugo (1990), McLaren (1985), Rockhill (1986), Thompson (1983), and Warren (1990). This chapter draws on
the work of these authors. In particular, our focus is on how gender, viewed
as an issue and as an expression of power, is organized and reproduced in
the learning environments provided by adult education institutions.

We begin with a definition of the term *gender*. We then consider the
societal environment within which both women and educational institutions exist. We explore the areas of politics, work, and violence to understand the sex or gender system in our society. We next move to more
specific analyses of some ways in which gender relations are experienced
within educational institutions. For illustrative purposes, we examine the
institutional environment, curricula, classroom conduct, and teacher-learner
relationships. We conclude with some recommendations for bringing about
more equitable learning environments for women.

Our discussion of these issues is illustrative rather than exhaustive in
nature. That is, it is based on our lived experiences and those of our women
friends and highlights only a few of the ways in which both societal and institutional learning contexts devalue and disempower women. Moreover, space
limitations do not permit a discussion of similarities of conduct in such settings
as industrial training, continuing medical education, and military education.

NEW DIRECTIONS FOR ADULT AND CONTINUING EDUCATION, no. 50, Summer 1991 © Jossey-Bass Inc., Publishers

## Defining Gender

It is generally acknowledged that "gender" is not a substitute term for "sex." While we are born into fairly unambiguous sexual categories (female and male) and while our gender (feminine and masculine) is usually ascribed on the basis of our sex, gender more properly refers to sociocultural interpretation of, and norms and values attached to, sexual differences. Guided by these ascriptions, we go on to live our lives on the basis of gender definitions that are arbitrarily tied to sexual differences.

Social conventions both define and legitimate what is considered "normal" and "natural" for one's sex or gender, with an emphasis on the differences between the sexes rather than on their common characteristics. Because gender characteristics are ascribed in polarized ways—to be masculine is not to be feminine—identification with one set of characteristics precludes identification with the other.

If gender were simply about differences, we probably would not be writing this chapter. However, there is an aspect of gender that is problematic. Social and cultural understandings of sexual differences are related to the oppression and exploitation of women. As we explore in the following discussion, these understandings allocate the privileges of status, power, and authority according to sex and gender differences: Masculine characteristics, attitudes, beliefs, and behaviors are valued as the norm, and the feminine counterparts are devalued. Men are empowered, women are disempowered.

## Women and Gender in Society

Women's experiences in the learning environments of educational institutions cannot be separated from their experiences within the wider society. The polarization and differentiation noted above are imbedded within social structures, and they affect women both in their daily lives and as learners. Indeed, institutional learning environments are both created by and mirror these broader societal patterns. Thus, the interrelationship among women, gender, and society is basic to a discussion of women and the learning environments provided by institutions.

The experiences women have in society are neither accidental nor incidental. A sex/gender system exists and it organizes relations between individuals and between the sexes in distinctive ways. Although there may be variations across historical periods, and variations or divisions along ethnic, racial, or class lines about what is appropriate to one's gender, common features exist. Consistently, the sex/gender system devalues the feminine while valuing the masculine and disempowers women while empowering men.

This system most often associates the feminine with the private sphere in our society—the familial, domestic, and apolitical. The masculine, by contrast, is associated with the public sphere in our society—patriarchal, political, and oriented to full-time paid work. This dichotomous conception that allocates men and women to different spheres is central to a sex/gender system. Such thinking affects the organization of society, the institutions and individuals within society, and our expectations of these institutions and individuals.

It is useful at this point to illustrate some ways in which women experience the sex/gender system in the wider society. While there is a significant and growing body of literature on this issue, we examine only three areas of women's lives: politics, work, and violence. We explore how a gender system assigns women and men to separate spheres and how, if taken for granted as "natural," this allocation then provides "explanations" about women's being and behavior.

**Women and Politics.** In exploring the political overtones of women's experiences, we are concerned with two interrelated meanings of the term *politics*. First, we are referring to formal politics, or the formal governmental organization. Second, we associate the term more broadly with issues of power, control, and authority.

A central problem in looking at women and politics is the definition of what constitutes political experience. For example, frequently, "women's issues" are defined as moral rather than political concerns (Siltanen and Stanworth, 1984). Consequently, issues of significance to women are not necessarily addressed by formal politics and politicians in the public arena. This problem of interpreting the political is compounded by the scarcity of women within formal politics and by the lower rates at which they participate in politics. This differential level of participation is the result of a political agenda that excludes women's issues and restricts women's power, control, and authority in society. Thus, this allocation of women and women's issues to a sphere that is separate from that of men fosters polarization between the sexes at the same time that it disempowers women. As discussed shortly, this scenario is repeated in institutional learning environments.

**Women and Work.** Women's relationship to work is another useful illustration of the ways in which women occupy a separate and less valued sphere. Analogous to politics, the definition of work is an issue. Feminist writers frequently point out that the interpretation of work as paid employment in the work force is misleading since it ignores women's unpaid domestic labor. Some feminist authors also argue that such undervaluation occurs because women's work in the home is seen as an extension of women's "natural" nurturing capacities and inclinations.

Some authors discuss the ways in which certain "women's work" presumes and draws on a certain type of sexualized femininity or on characteristics categorized as feminine (Connell, 1987; Stanko, 1988). It follows that those women who work in "nontraditional" areas are few in number and are seen to violate a "natural order" (Cockburn, 1985). Increasingly, women are seen to violate a natural order simply by entering the workplace, and this breach of "proper" behavior is being met by violence. In the United States from 1980 to 1985, 42 percent of women killed at work were murdered. This compares to 2 percent of men ("Alarm Over Workplace Murders," 1990). As noted later, this "gendering" of the work world into separate women's and men's spheres is parallelled, and supported, by a gendering of the learning environment.

**Women and Violence.** While some might suggest that violence is not an area of women's experiences in the same way as are politics and work, we view violence against women as an area that subsumes all others, as indicated at least in part by the above-cited statistics on women murdered in the workplace. Analysis of women's relationship to violence clearly illustrates how women and their concerns are disempowered and devalued in both obvious and subtle ways.

There are many studies that detail the extent to which obvious forms of violence against women occur. For example, in the United States it is estimated that over 1.5 million women are physically assaulted by a partner each year (Browne, 1987). Although this kind of statistic clearly speaks to the existence of violence in women's experiences, it is important to realize, most researchers acknowledge, that women underreport violence against them. We do know, however, that such violence is a problem in all socio-economic, ethnic, and religious groups.

Less obvious, but equally problematic, is the issue of sexual harassment in women's lives (Stanko, 1988). Indeed, violence against women can be seen as all-pervasive if we take into consideration the images in media and popular culture that present women in highly objectified ways or as passive ornaments for consumption by the male gaze (Bartky, 1988; Bordo, 1990; Dworkin, 1981).

This kind of violence clearly illustrates the allocation of women and men to separate spheres. So, too, does the gender-based difference in remediation. Inasmuch as the private sphere, associated with the feminine, familial, and domestic, is defined as outside the arena of political intervention, violence against women can be ignored by those within the public sphere. Indeed, many governments refuse to pass legislation on issues such as domestic violence.

Thus, when women enter institutional learning environments, they have already learned about what is "normal" and "natural" from their experiences in the wider social context. Most adult women learners not only have learned the lessons of the gender-based double standard in U.S. society, but they also have learned how to survive in that hostile climate. These survival strategies are required in institutional learning environments as well. Unfortunately, those settings both mirror society at large and create similarly hostile contexts for women learners.

## Women and Gender in Educational Institutions

What happens to women in society happens to women learners in institutional learning environments at two levels. First, the larger institutional environment mirrors the characteristics of the broader social environment. Second, and more important, educational institutions produce and reproduce the sex/gender system. Although its production and reproduction happens in many ways, we briefly focus here only on the interrelated areas of curricula, classroom conduct, and teacher-learner interactions.

**Institutional Environment.** Within educational institutions, as within the wider society, women still occupy a separate sphere. In terms of paid work in some institutions, women tend to occupy different and lower administrative positions in educational bureaucracies than those that men occupy. The workplace participation of women continues to be concentrated primarily in service rather than administrative positions. They operate in traditionally "female" positions such as cleaning, catering, and clerical work. Rarely are they seen in the higher reaches of administration, research, and teaching (Ramazanogl, 1987).

Like the wider society, educational institutions provide locations for violence against women. The 1990 Montreal massacre of fourteen young engineering women students by a man who first condemned them as "feminists" is a vivid and poignant illustration of the consequences of entering what some perceive as nontraditional areas and violating a "natural order." A more subtle form of violence, sexual harassment, also occurs within educational institutions. At Cornell University, for example, 60 percent of women students reported having been sexually harassed at the institution (Gabriel and Smithson, 1990). Gender-based harassment is not restricted to students. Backhouse, Harris, Michelle, and Wylie (1989) detail the existence of a "chilly climate" for faculty members as well. This chilly climate within institutional environments is intensified for women learners through male-dominated curricula, classroom conduct, and teacher-learner interactions.

**Curricula.** It is important to understand that curricula are not simply neutral selections and presentations of knowledge (Griffin, 1983). Curricula are expressions and reflections of what we consider worth knowing. As such, they legitimate certain areas of information and knowledge while they exclude others. Generally, what is considered worthwhile knowledge has been described as knowledge by, for, and about men. In the history of adult education, for example, while we devote a considerable amount of time to charting the progress of male adult educators and male-dominated organizations, we have not devoted a corresponding amount of time to the stories of women adult educators and the organizations in which women were prominent (Hugo, 1990).

In most adult education curricula, there is an absence of women, women's concerns, and feminist literature that might provide a basis from which women learners could begin to articulate, present, and theorize about their experiences (Walker, n.d.). This avoidance of women's concerns is complemented by texts that characterize women in stereotypical ways, that is, ways that at least implicitly position women in the domestic sphere and in unauthoritative roles. For example, in one adult education text (Houle, 1972) analyzed by Collard (1990), out of a total of twenty-two roles mentioned in the first fifty pages, only five were used with the pronoun "she." Women were described as broadening their interests, as home economists teaching low-income mothers, as secretaries, and as typing teachers. In contrast, men were ascribed not only more roles, but those roles covered a much broader range from tutor to director. What is important to realize is that this text (even though it is nearly twenty years old) legitimizes a covert message that devalues and disempowers women when used as a reference for or by adult educators.

Moreover, among adult education studies that consider sex as a major variable, there is a tendency to cast in stone what differences do exist and to view females as aberrant or deficient when and where they fail to comply with male "norms." Alternately, some research is centered on males, but results are treated as generalizable to the population. Often these circumstances are hidden in texts that cite researchers' works without noting the sex of their respondents. For example, the research work of London, Wenkert, and Hagstrom (1963) on participation and social class is often cited as a classic. However, the fact that the sample was exclusively male is seldom noted.

Given these characteristics of the curricula, it is important to examine precisely what women learn, or what can they learn, from curricula and texts that ignore their lives and experiences. Often such curricula and texts even cast that experience in highly conventional and trivialized ways. As Benhabib (1990) suggests, "gender" can be used as a theoretical term that both sensitizes us to certain kinds of differences and helps focus our attention on the social and cultural constructions of sexual differences. If this analysis is correct, then the prevalence of maleness in the curricula ensures the existence of a learning environment that works to the detriment of women.

**Classroom Conduct.** Curricular problems are compounded by what can broadly be termed classroom conduct. While many adult educators now recognize the importance of using gender-neutral language in texts and in teaching, few recognize that the language, the ways that the language is used, and classroom discourse and conduct are interrelated. For example, the adversarial logic that dominates education institutions alienates many women learners (Moulton, 1983; Schweickart, 1990). This logic typically includes argument and counterargument, posture and pose, as integral parts of a demonstration of intellectual competence. These behaviors are reflected in and defined by frequent usage of militant, aggressive language, for example, words like *win, lose, battle, ammunition, defeat,* and *compete* (Kramerae and Treichler, 1990). As Belenky, Clinchy, Goldberger, and Tarule (1986) suggest, these ways of being or conversing are outside of women's usual and preferred ways of reaching understandings and coming to "know" their worlds.

One possible outcome of the mismatch between classroom conduct and women's ways of knowing is silencing. Warren (1990) suggests that silencing may be an adaptation to a situation of perceived powerlessness by the learners, even among women who can display a mastery of knowledge.

With respect to classroom discourse, part of the "problem" for women learners involves their progress toward thinking, reading, writing, and talking "like a man." That is, while acquiring the skills and knowledge needed to demonstrate their intellectual abilities, women may have to "defeminize" their ways of knowing. They may become distant from their preferred, female ways of learning and knowing. In doing so, they become "denatured," that is, they depart from the socially sanctioned norms of what it is to be a woman. Consequently, to be a successful woman learner and to achieve in educational institutions is to somehow not be a woman.

In summary, within educational institutions the criteria for acquiring and demonstrating learning and knowledge of the curricula emphasize a "masculine" mastery. In contrast, criteria that emphasize a display of comfortable familiarity with knowledge and information, acquired through ways more appropriate to women's ways of knowing, would foster the valuing and empowerment of women learners.

**Teacher-Learner Interactions.** There is a considerable amount of literature indicating that teachers give qualitatively different evaluations and feedback to girls than is given to boys (Stanworth, 1983). The dominant message in elementary and high schools continues into the adult learning environment (Butterwick, Collard, Gray, and Kastner, 1990). Through teacher-learner interactions, women, like girls, learn that their achievements depend on care and compliance with formal rules and that their failures result from inadequate intellectual abilities. The structures of the teacher-learner interactions in essence "teach" learners about male dominance. In other words, differential patterns of social constraints and privileges are experienced by women and men. Who gets to talk, who interrupts, and whose comments are acknowledged all indicate to women learners that the nature of teacher-learner interactions is gender-related (Kramerae and Treichler, 1990; Lewis and Simon, 1986; Spender, 1980a, 1980b).

This differential treatment of men and women is explicit in situations where teachers make comments clearly tied to women's sexuality or allocate rewards to women students who act according to "normal" female gender characteristics. Most pernicious are those instructors who require, and draw on for their own support, the stereotypical "feminine" qualities of nurturance and support. Such interactions in some situations might be termed collegial. However, in learning environments within institutional settings, there are power differences between the instructor and the student that cannot be ignored and that can change the tenor of the interactions from that of friendship to that of harassment.

Teacher-learner interactions are further confused by the different expectations of male versus female instructors. Often, there is an expectation that women teachers will be more nurturing. At the same time, they are frequently evaluated by students as less authoritative in terms of content and processes if they perform in ways congruent with women's ways of being and knowing (Backhouse, Harris, Michelle, and Wylie, 1989; Kramerae and Treichler, 1990). In the context of educational institutions dominated by masculine ways of being and thinking, such evaluation disparities are not unexpected.

## Recommendations

Although this chapter has dealt only briefly with a complex subject, the aim has been to point out some of the dilemmas in the interrelationship of women, gender, and learning environments that exist in educational institutions. Resolution of these problems can be approached in two ways. We could focus on women learners and the activities required for them to alter their devaluation and disempowerment. But this type of approach is not consistent with the direction of this chapter because the approach suggests that women learners are more likely to accommodate than resist their situation. Moreover, it treats women learners as somehow not "normal" and requiring remediation. In effect, it blames the victims.

Rather than focus on women learners and steps they might take to resolve these issues, we believe that a focus on adult educators is a more promising approach to addressing inequities in the learning environment. Adult educators can choose to ignore the hostile learning environments that women face in institutional settings. Alternately and more usefully, adult educators need to respond to gender-based discrimination at individual, institutional, and societal levels.

As individuals, adult educators must begin to take personal responsibility for understanding the issues and concerns relevant to women learners. In the last twenty years, a myriad of articles, books, and monographs have been written about these issues and concerns. Nonetheless, some educators continue to treat these matters as more appropriate for the coffee room than for the classroom. Educators must begin to examine their own daily behaviors. They must ask of themselves, their colleagues, and their learners the question, "In what ways do I disempower and devalue women learners?" And they must act constructively on the responses.

Obviously, educators can pursue, as part of their programs, content and instructional processes that are appropriate to women learners. They can foster dialogue on women's issues at all levels of practice, theory, and research. They can implement techniques that ensure sufficient time and space are available for women to identify their own concerns and develop their own strategies. These recommendations are not simple ones, however. Both adult educators and learners may not be sufficiently aware of gender issues to be able to undertake these processes productively. Further, if not handled sensitively and appropriately, specific dialogue or techniques may inadvertently suggest that women learners are passive recipients rather than active players in the discourse. Nonetheless, progress can be made and it is worth the effort to try to increase the value and power of women learners (see Lewis and Simon, 1986).

Although the sensitivities and endeavors of individual adult educators are laudable, individual goodwill is not a sufficiently effective response to the current situation of many women learners. Adult educators need to work within institutional learning environments that facilitate their efforts for positive change. Institutions that have a serious concern for women learners must make structural changes to ensure that women and women's issues are considered. They must shift their concern from equal accessibility and opportunity to equal outcomes for women. Such a shift requires that firm policies be established in cooperation with women learners and administrators. Clearly stated goals for the institutions, explicit timelines, and supporting rewards and sanctions are needed.

Individual and institutional efforts can improve institutional learning environments for women. However, within institutional settings such solutions are not totally satisfactory, for the issue of gender is embedded within broader societal structures. Ultimately, changes must extend to all levels of society to ensure that women's learning activities are conducted within the broader context of a society that is supportive and validating. The implementation of such changes is a complex process. It requires adult educators to facilitate and lobby for political changes that empower and value women. Adult educators also must foster the involvement of women in both formal governmental organizations and in the processes of power, control, and authority.

## Conclusion

Increasingly, adult educators are becoming familiar with the issues of women, gender, and the learning environment. Certainly, the concerns raised in this chapter are not new. They have existed in Western societies since the mid-1800s when women attempted to enter male-dominated educational institutions. Intellectual understanding of the need for gender-neutral learning environments, however, is not the same as creating gender-neutral learning environments. The establishment of these environments requires us, as adult educators, to accept the responsibility for conducting ourselves in ways that display a genuine commitment to women learners.

## References

"Alarm Over Workplace Murders." *Calgary Herald,* Dec. 5, 1990.
Backhouse, C., Harris, R., Michelle, G., and Wylie, A. "The Chill Climate for Faculty at UWO: Postscript to the Backhouse Report." Unpublished manuscript, University of Western Ontario, London, Ontario, Canada, 1989.
Bartky, S. L. "Foucault, Femininity, and the Modernization of Patriarchal Power." In I. Diamond and L. Quinby (eds.), *Feminism and Foucault: Reflections on Resistance.* Boston: Northeastern University Press, 1988.
Belenky, M. F., Clinchy, N., Goldberger, L., and Tarule, J. M. *Women's Ways of Knowing: The Development of Self, Voice, and Mind.* New York: Basic Books, 1986.
Benhabib, S. "On Contemporary Feminist Theory." *Dissent,* 1990, *36,* 367–378.
Bordo, S. "Reading the Slender Body." In M. Jacobus, E. Fox Keller, and S. Shuttleworth (eds.), *Body/Politics: Women and the Discourses of Science.* New York: Routledge & Kegan Paul, 1990.
Browne, A. *When Battered Women Kill.* New York: Free Press, 1987.
Butterwick, S., Collard, S., Gray, J., and Kastner, A. "Soul Search and Research." In *Proceedings of the 1990 Canadian Association for the Study of Adult Education Conference.* Victoria, British Columbia, Canada: University of Victoria, 1990.
Cockburn, C. *Machinery of Dominance.* London, England: Pluto Press, 1985.
Collard, S. "Feminism and the Sociology of Science." Paper presented to Graduate Program of Adult Continuing Education, Northern Illinois University, 1990.
Connell, R. W. *Gender and Power: Society, the Person, and Sexual Politics.* Stanford, Calif.: Stanford University Press, 1987.
Dworkin, A. *Our Blood: Prophecies and Discourses on Sexual Politics.* New York: Putnam, 1981.
Gabriel, S. L., and Smithson, I. (eds.). *Gender in the Classroom: Power and Pedagogy.* Urbana: University of Illinois Press, 1990.
Griffin, C. *Curriculum Theory in Adult and Lifelong Education.* London, England: Croom-Helm, 1983.
Hayes, E. R., and Smith, L. "The Impact of Feminism on Adult Education: An Analysis of Trends in Scholarship." In *Proceedings of the Annual Adult Education Research Conference.* Athens: University of Georgia, 1990.
Houle, C. O. *The Design of Education.* San Francisco: Jossey-Bass, 1972.
Hughes, M., and Kennedy, M. "Breaking Out: Women in Adult Education." *Women's Studies International Forum,* 1980, *6,* 261–269.
Hugo, J. M. "Adult Education History and the Issue of Gender: Toward a Different History of Adult Education in America." *Adult Education Quarterly,* 1990, *41,* 1–16.
Kramerae, C., and Treichler, P. "Power Relationships in the Classroom." In S. L. Gabriel and I. Smithson (eds.), *Gender in the Classroom: Power and Pedagogy.* Urbana: University of Illinois, 1990.
Lewis, M., and Simon, R. I. "A Discourse Not Intended for Her: Learning and Teaching Within Patriarchy." *Harvard Educational Review,* 1986, *56,* 457–472.
London, J., Wenkert, R., and Hagstrom, W. *Adult Education and Social Class.* Berkeley: Survey Research Center, University of California, 1963.
McLaren, A. *Ambitions and Realizations: Women in Adult Education.* London, England: Peter Owen, 1985.

Moulton, J. "A Paradigm of Philosophy: The Adversary Method." In S. Harding and M. Hintikka (eds.), *Discovering Reality*. Dordrecht, The Netherlands: D. Reidel, 1983.

Ramazanogl, C. "Sex and Violence in Academic Life or You Can Keep a Good Woman Down." In J. Hamer and M. Maynard (eds.), *Women, Violence, and Social Control*. Atlantic Highlands, N.J.: Humanities Press, 1987.

Rockhill, K. "Literacy as Threat/Desire: Longing to Be Somebody." In J. Gaskell and A. McLaren (eds.), *Women and Education*. Calgary, Albert, Canada: Detselig Enterprises, 1986.

Schweickart, P. "Reading, Teaching, and the Ethic of Care." In S. L. Gabriel and I. Smithson (eds.), *Gender in the Classroom: Power and Pedagogy*. Urbana: University of Illinois, 1990.

Siltanen, J., and Stanworth, M. (eds.). *Women and the Public Sphere: A Critique of Sociology and Politics*. New York: St. Martin's Press, 1984.

Spender, D. "Learning to Create Our Own Knowledge." *Convergence*, 1980a, *13* (1–2), 14–22.

Spender, D. *Man-Made Language*. London, England: Routledge & Kegan Paul, 1980b.

Stanko, E. "Keeping Women In and Out of Line: Sexual Harassment and Occupational Segregation." In S. Walby (ed.), *Gender Segregation at Work*. Milton Keynes, England: Open University Press, 1988.

Stanworth, M. *Gender and Schooling*. London, England: Hutchinson, 1983.

Thompson, J. *Learning Liberation: Women's Responses to Men's Education*. London, England: Croom-Helm, 1983.

Walker, G. "Written with Invisible Ink: Women in the Adult Education Knowledge Base." Unpublished manuscript, Carleton University, Ottawa, Ontario, n.d.

Warren, C. "Review of Belenky et al." *Canadian Journal for the Study of Adult Education*, 1990, *4* (1), 63–67.

*Susan Collard is a doctoral student completing her research at the University of British Columbia, Vancouver, Canada. Her research interests are in the areas of feminism and critical theory.*

*Joyce Stalker is assistant professor of continuing education at the University of Calgary, Alberta, Canada. Her research interests are in the areas of equity and the sociology of adult education.*

*Both authors have been regular contributors to and active participants in adult education conferences in Canada and the United States.*

*Considerable information is available pertaining to adult learning environments.*

# Resources on Adult Learning Environments

*Rodney D. Fulton, Roger Hiemstra*

The chapters in this volume contain information on various aspects of the learning environment. Some of these aspects focus on actions an adult educator can take to make changes or improvements in the environment, such as addressing a physical space limitation or trying to understand what an individual is experiencing as a learner. Other aspects focus on perceptions, beliefs, and attitudes, such as trying to understand how personal views about race, gender, or technology affect the activities of teaching and interacting with adults.

This resources chapter provides additional information on all of these aspects. Some resource suggestions cover quite concrete material where direct applications are possible in an adult teaching and learning situation. Other citations provide background information for the reader interested in analyzing and reflecting on personal views. Still other citations provide some basic understanding of crucial societal and cultural issues. Although some of the resources are most likely not the typical fare read by busy adult education professionals, we recommend a broad-based approach to studying the topics presented in this volume.

In addition to books, we cite several monographs and journal articles containing seminal information. Although there is some overlap, most of the references shown at the conclusion of each chapter have not been annotated here. We encourage readers to consult those sources as well in the interest of promoting greater self-understanding among adult educators. It our hope that critical reflection, dialogue, and knowledge development are stimulated by this volume.

## Books

Agger, B. *Socio(onto)logy: A Disciplinary Reading.* Chicago: University of Illinois Press, 1989.

While "heavy" in content (several sections require two or three readings for full comprehension), this book is a good source for the adult educator who is struggling to understand learning environments in the light of such sociological terms or concepts as positivism, heuristics, modernity, postmodernism, hegemony, hermeneutics, and radical feminism. Various authors with critical theory or Marxist views are discussed, including Theodor Adorno, Michael Foucault, and Jurgen Habermas.

Ashcraft, N., and Scheflen, A. E. *People Space: The Making and Breaking of Human Boundaries.* Garden City, N.Y.: Anchor, 1976.

The book examines how people use space in various contexts. The authors also provide some perspectives on how individuals' territorial views affect their uses of space. There are chapters on such topics as privacy, defense, crowding, and violence, which are important if we are to correctly and creatively use space for effective learning.

Belenky, M. F., Clinchy, N., Goldberger, L., and Tarule, J. M. *Women's Ways of Knowing: The Development of Self, Voice, and Mind.* New York: Basic Books, 1986.

This book has perhaps done more than any other to "popularize" and help promote the new understanding that many women learn in ways different than those of men. Based on interviews with both students and women in professional roles, five distinct categories for "knowing" emerged: (1) a position of silence, subject to the whim of authority, (2) received knowledge from others, (3) subjective knowledge often associated with an inner voice, (4) procedural knowledge involving learning how to apply objective means for acquiring and communicating information, and (5) constructed knowledge where women view themselves as knowledge creators. Several ideas for fostering women's development in learning situations are presented.

Bulkin, E. *Yours in Struggle: Three Feminist Perspectives on Anti-Semitism and Racism.* New York: Long Haul Press, 1984.

This book provides essays from three feminists—Elly Bulkin, Minnie Bruce Pratt, and Barbara Smith—who present Jewish, black, and white southern views on such topics as racism, feminism, lesbianism, and anti-Semitism. The book is especially helpful for the male adult educator struggling to understand various feminist views so he can improve his educational efforts.

Castaldi, B. *Educational Facilities: Planning, Modernization, and Management.* (3rd ed.) Newton, Mass.: Allyn & Bacon, 1987.

Written as a textbook for public school administrators, the process described in this book, from preplanning to postconstruction, actually is applicable to all educational facilities. Brief mention is made of extended uses of school facilities for other community uses.

Gilligan, C. *In a Different Voice: Psychological Theory and Women's Development.* Cambridge, Mass.: Harvard University Press, 1982.

Gilligan was one of the first American authors to discuss distinctive developmental characteristics of women. Although focusing primarily on moral development issues, there is much in this book about adult development in general that the interested adult education practitioner should consider.

Gueulette, D. G. (ed.). *Microcomputers for Adult Learning.* Chicago: Follett, 1982.

This book was the first to present a comprehensive review of how microcomputer technology affects adult learning. A variety of chapters describe how the technology can be used in adult education. Several ideas and implications for designing effective learning environments with microcomputers are presented.

Lapides, F. R., and Burrows, D. J. (eds.). *Racism: A Casebook.* New York: Crowell, 1971.

This book contains fourteen essays and six short stories. Authors such as James Baldwin, Alex Haley, Ann Petry, John Williams, and Malcolm X present information or views related to racism, prejudices, and stereotypes. This book provides good background information, especially for white adult educators, on these topics.

Leed, K., and Leed, J. *Building for Adult Learning.* Cincinnati, Ohio: Leed Design Associates, 1987.

Taking a cookbook approach, the authors offer several specific examples, with written and photographic documentation, of how to design appropriate places for adult learning. Grounded in a systems approach to design, a five-step model of physical environment design goals is offered, including meeting creature comforts, creating a climate of trust and sharing, maximizing social contacts, enhancing high quality, and inspiring greater achievement. Although the authors are architects, they incorporate several basic principles of adult learning in their work.

Moos, R. H. *Evaluating Educational Environments: Procedures, Measures, Findings, and Policy Implications.* San Francisco: Jossey-Bass, 1979.

A model for understanding interactions between the individual and the environment is presented, incorporating three aspects: design of physical space, organizational attributes, and group characteristics. Moos suggests that these aspects of interaction affect the social environment, which in turn affects student participation, satisfaction, and living patterns. This book includes important information on the Classroom Environment Scale that is useful to adult educators.

Sleeman, P., and Rockwell, D. (eds.). *Designing Learning Environments.* New York: Longman, 1981.

The editors have attempted to compile a comprehensive work on the design of learning environments but admit that no single work can exhaust the topic. Cautioning readers that the single most important component is the learner, Sleeman and Rockwell include chapters on traditional topics such as site selection, noise factors, and financing; however, they also address technology, media, and staff training in relation to design. They suggest the need for learning environment consultants. This book is out-of-print but worth the effort of locating it in a library collection.

Sommer, R. *Tight Spaces: Hard Architecture and How to Humanize It.* Englewood Cliffs, N.J.: Prentice-Hall, 1974.

This book contains chapters related to such topics as hard architecture, movable chairs, crowding, and sociopetal/sociofugal arrangements. Ideas for arranging learning environments are presented.

Takaki, R. (ed.). *From Different Shores: Perspectives on Race and Ethnicity in America.* New York: Oxford University Press, 1987.

The editor brings together a wide range of contemporary essays on the nature and meaning of America's social diversity. Such questions as the following are addressed: How have the experiences of various racial minorities been similar and different? Is "race" the same as "ethnicity"? How has culture shaped race and ethnic relations? How can racial and gender issues be compared? This is an important book to read in order to increase personal sensitivity to racial, ethnic, and gender-based issues that affect the learning environment.

Tannen, D. *You Just Don't Understand: Women and Men in Conversation.* New York: William Morrow, 1990.

This book helps us to better understand some of the sociolinguistic differences between men and women that can affect learning environments. Recent research from linguistic and social sciences that indicates how women and men use language differently is included. Men see themselves as autonomous individuals, where conversations are attempts to achieve and maintain an upper hand. Women see themselves as enmeshed in a web of relationships that they want to maintain, and conversations are negotiations for closeness, confirmation, and support.

## Book Chapters, Journal Articles, and Monographs

Finkel, C. "The 'Total Immersion' Meeting Environment." *Training and Development Journal*, 1980, *34* (9), 32–39.

Using the training "meeting" as the unit for discussion, Finkel details the requirements for a successful meeting, one in which the learners can spend all of their time on task. He details the physical components that allow an employee to become a totally immersed learner.

Finkel, C. "Where Learning Happens." *Training and Development Journal*, 1984, *38* (4), 32–36.

While Skinnerian in his approach to the relationship of place to learning, Finkel acknowledges that both the leader's and the participants' points of view are vital in designing successful learning. He claims that the environment must support physical, intellectual, and psychological needs of both learners and instructors.

Fulton, R. *Importance of Place to Adult Learning*. Columbus: ERIC Clearinghouse on Adult, Career, and Vocational Education, Ohio State University, 1991. (ED 324 420)

This work summarizes the history of adult educators who have tried to determine the interrelationships between physical environment and adult learning. The document also highlights several attempts to bring the physical environment to the attention of adult educators in the United States. A comprehensive bibliography of architectural, educational, psychological, and sociological sources is included.

Goulette, G. "Physical Factors to Consider When Training Adults." *Training and Development Journal*, 1970, *24* (7), 40–43.

This article deals with the concept that the declining physical abilities of aging learners should be accommodated through necessary alterations of the physical learning environment. The article concentrates on sight and sound but includes other factors to be considered when changing the environment to meet adult learners' needs.

Hayes, E. R. "Insights from Women's Experiences for Teaching and Learning." In E. R. Hayes (ed.), *Effective Teaching Styles*. New Directions for Adult and Continuing Education, no. 43. San Francisco: Jossey-Bass, 1989.

Hayes presents a rationale for a feminist pedagogy and describes what the corresponding process should entail: collaboration in teaching and learning activities, cooperative communication styles, holistic approaches to learning, strategies for theory building, and action projects. She urges consideration of these strategies in the light of women's needs as learners, and appreciation of women's strengths and experiences.

Hiemstra, R., and Sisco, B. "Physical Learning Environment." In R. Hiemstra and B. Sisco (eds.), *Individualizing Instruction: Making Learning Personal, Empowering, and Successful.* San Francisco: Jossey-Bass, 1990.

This article in the book's resources section attempts to be comprehensive in examining the physical environment, since the authors feel that it has been largely overlooked in the literature. Sections on anthropometry, ergonomics, proxemics, and synaesthetics are designed to raise adult educators' levels of awareness so that they can create learning settings that are maximally optimal for learning. Hiemstra and Sisco raise important questions but do not dictate answers. Rather, they give the readers tools with which to develop their own answers.

Hinton, B. "Set the Stage for Student Success." *Lifelong Learning,* 1985, *9* (2), 29–30.

This short article offers concrete suggestions for achieving student success, such as adequate lighting, comfortable temperature, appropriate bulletin boards, informal seating, and the opportunity for individual study carrels. Rearrangement of the physical environment along with other suggested activities encourages success for all students, no matter how varied their individual needs.

Hugo, J. M. "Adult Education History and the Issue of Gender: Toward a Different History of Adult Education in America." *Adult Education Quarterly,* 1990, *41,* 1–16.

Hugo argues that historians have marginalized or written women out of the historical narrative of the adult education field. She believes that historians must take a compensatory approach to women's marginal status and suggests that the interrelationships of gender, race, and class must be better understood. The adult education teacher who is interested in promoting an enhanced learning environment for all learners will find the article provocative and disturbing because of the many changes needed and their implications.

Kolodny, A. "Colleges Must Recognize Students' Cognitive Styles and Cultural Backgrounds." *Chronicle of Higher Education,* Feb. 6, 1991, p. A44.

Kolodny explains why educators must think about not only what they are teaching but also who and how. Although directed primarily at undergraduate teaching, she offers several ideas appropriate for adult education as well. She describes how high attrition rates for women in engineering courses were traced to teaching approaches that failed to account for the way women prefer to learn and discuss subject matter.

Lewis, M., and Simon, R. I. "A Discourse Not Intended for Her: Learning and Teaching Within Patriarchy." *Harvard Educational Review,* 1986, *56,* 457–472.

The experience of most women in American society involves being silenced, even in classrooms. In this article a female student and male teacher describe and analyze the process of silencing that takes place in learning settings. Men and women, whether as teacher or student, must struggle to find a common voice, to promote equality in the learning environment, and to reduce the gender-biased societal power of men.

Luttrell, W. "Working-Class Women's Ways of Knowing: Effects of Gender, Race, and Class." *Sociology of Education,* 1989, *62,* 33–46.

This article describes and analyzes how black and white working-class women use knowledge. These women's perspectives challenge feminist views of a universal mode of knowing for women. Instead, the author suggests that complex power relations of gender, race, and class exist that shape how women think, learn, and know. For adult educators concerned with creating equitable learning environments, the author suggests that ethnic, class, and race issues specific to women's experiences must be carefully examined.

Verner, C., and Davison, C. *Physiological Factors in Adult Learning and Instruction.* Tallahassee: Research Information Processing Center, Department of Adult Education, Florida State University, 1971.

This monograph was written for practitioners attempting to translate research into useable information for adult educators. The physiological condition of learners, especially vision, hearing, psychomotor skills, and memory, are discussed with a goal of encouraging adult educators to manage the learning environment skillfully, to accentuate a learner's physiological capabilities, and to compensate for deficiencies.

Vosko, R. S. "Shaping Spaces for Lifelong Learning." *Lifelong Learning,* 1984, *9* (1), 4–7, 28.

This article is based on the dual assumption that adult educators must be concerned with providing learning climates that support learning and that the physical aspects of those environments are important. Vosko discusses two important elements of the physical environment: personal distances and seating arrangements. By showing how different spaces and arrangements can facilitate or impede interactions among learners, the author clarifies the interrelationship between physical arrangements and learning activities.

Vosko, R. S., and Hiemstra, R. "The Adult Learning Environment: Importance of Physical Features." *International Journal of Lifelong Education*, 1988, 7, 185–195.

The authors review the literature on three topics germane to physical features of adult learning environments: ergonomics, anthropometry, and proxemics. While acknowledging that much more research is needed on these topics, Vosko and Hiemstra recommend that adult educators evaluate learners' needs in relation to the physical arrangements of the learning environment. The authors' aim is to encourage discussion and further research on this relatively unexplored subject.

Weinstein, C. "Classroom Design as an External Condition for Learning." *Educational Technology*, 1981, 21 (8), 12–19.

Stating that the design of a classroom is secondary to curriculum and instruction, Weinstein nevertheless suggests that the teacher can control at least furniture arrangement, seating position, and classroom aesthetics, all of which seem to affect student behavior and attitudes. She reviews research on classrooms organized by territory versus those organized by function and discusses aesthetics, noting that there is very little research on the topic. She supports the concept that teachers and instructional designers need to develop environmental competence and suggests ways to achieve that competence.

White, S. *Physical Criteria for Adult Learning Environments.* Washington, D.C.: Commission on Planning Adult Learning Systems, Facilities, and Environments, Adult Education Association of the U.S.A., 1972. (ED 080 882)

Often quoted for the claim that 25 percent of adult learning is directly attributable to the physical environment, the author attempted to gather together what little was known from various sources. White suggests that physical arrangements need to contribute to an "aura of adulthood." The author addresses how several physical attributes can create a "feeling of ease, confidence, and capability." An annotated bibliography supports the document.

Readers also are encouraged to review various back issues of *New Directions for Adult and Continuing Education* for a multitude of chapters related to some aspect of the learning environment.

*Rodney D. Fulton holds master's degrees in psychology and adult and higher education. He is adjunct instructor in the Department of Education and staff member in the College of Nursing, Montana State University, Bozeman.*

*Roger Hiemstra is professor of adult education and chair of the adult education program at Syracuse University, Syracuse, New York.*

*The previous chapters provide many challenging ideas and suggestions that can be used to guide practice, thinking, and research related to building more effective learning environments.*

# Toward Building More Effective Learning Environments

*Roger Hiemstra*

The task of understanding the multiple aspects of learning environments and then attempting to make these environments more effective is a complex undertaking. It requires that professional adult educators look not only at the physical spaces in which learning takes place but also at the attitudes, perceptions, and beliefs that they and participating learners bring to educational settings. Often a perspective transformation, paradigm shift, or reassessment of a personal philosophy is needed, as noted in Chapter One.

Expansion of our personal awareness of various issues associated with learning environments depends on a willingness to consider new ideas and approaches. This means listening to the many "voices" that address the issues, being open to change in our personal practices, and raising new questions about teaching and learning. In other words, I hope that much more takes place than just the passive participation of reading this volume. I hope some "deeper understandings" will be achieved through critical reflections on the content of the chapters presented here.

## What Constitutes the Learning Environment?

This volume brings together the thinking and experiences of several people to examine issues associated with learning environments. In Chapter One, I outline some of my own growth in understanding learning environments as a demonstration of the complexities involved, at least for me. I also provide my current definition of the learning environment and suggest that there are at least three ways we can think about the various changes needed to build more effective environments. In this final chapter I present information on the kinds of research and changes in practice needed if we are going to make learning environments more effective.

One necessary consideration is the selection, design, or manipulation of the physical spaces in which learning takes place. In Chapter Two, Rodney D. Fulton outlines his model (SPATIAL) of some of the relationships between various components of a physical space. In Chapter Three, Richard S. Vosko applies his experience as a space and design specialist to the topic of the physical learning environment and urges us to become much more cognizant of the way people actually use space. Judith K. DeJoy, in Chapter Four, describes the complexities involved in designing micro-computer systems that meet at least some of the emotional and perceptual needs of learners.

The second aspect of the learning environment addressed in this volume pertains to the psychological or emotional climate of the learning environment. Burton R. Sisco, in Chapter Five, builds a case for the importance of the first encounter between instructor and learners in building an effective climate for learning. In Chapter Six, V. L. Mike Mahoney is concerned with the internal and external baggage a learner carries into the learning environment; he provides some recommendations for what instructors can do to help learners overcome these barriers.

A third aspect of the learning environment concerns the social and cultural complexities that practitioners and learners face as they undertake educational experiences. In Chapter Seven, Scipio A. J. Colin III and Trudie Kibbe Preciphs argue that racism generally has not been confronted by adult educators, and, as a result, learning environment effectiveness for many people is severely limited. A similar theme regarding disempowerment of women by many adult educators is explored by Susan Collard and Joyce Stalker in Chapter Eight. Both of these chapters are written to stimulate "real" soul searching and, hopefully, a new commitment to women, blacks, and other racial and ethnic minorities.

## Commitments to New Practices

The information contained in this volume suggests that adult educators must make several new commitments if the learning environment is to be improved. For some of us, this process of improvement will entail examination of our daily behavior to see if we inadvertently practice techniques or administer policies that in effect inhibit certain learners. Others of us may need to confront the bureaucracy or traditions in our institutions that somehow diminish learning environment effectiveness by impeding learners and teachers.

Several ideas, guidelines, and practical suggestions are provided by the volume's authors. As a summary, I highlight here some of the recommendations for changing and improving practice.

*Helping Learners Control the Learning Environment.* Many adult educators today are advocates of this notion of helping learners take more responsibility for and assume more control of their own learning. Several volume
authors detail how to empower learners, help them become more aware of
the environment, and help them take control of or change troublesome
environmental features.

*Analyzing and Controlling the Physical Space.* A number of questions can
be asked and actions taken to examine and evaluate the actual physical
spaces in which teaching and learning take place. Fulton and Vosko suggest
several actions to determine the appropriateness of space and furnishings
within the classroom, and Vosko recommends space "audits." Educators
should regularly check to see if any space-related problems have developed.
It is important to ask whether or not the space can be redesigned or
rearranged for sociopetal relationships.

*Incorporating Microcomputer Technology into Learning Environments.* The
increasingly user-friendly nature of microcomputers, their diminishing
costs, and their growing pervasiveness in society make them more and
more attractive as teaching and learning aids. DeJoy provides several criteria for evaluating and choosing microcomputers, including applicability,
available documentation, interactive capabilities, and flexibility. Careful
planning should take place prior to the incorporation of microcomputers
into the adult learning environment.

*Working with Learners.* Several practical suggestions are provided by
various authors on how to work effectively with learners. Sisco describes
several preparatory activities for the first meeting with learners and lists
helpful questions to ask about the first session. Mahoney recommends
getting to know learners and the problems that they face. He also suggests
specific actions such as using job-related or community-based learning
activities where appropriate.

*Helping Learners Feel at Ease.* Sisco describes several icebreakers that can
be used to help learners become acquainted, feel more at ease, and diminish
feelings of formality that often exist in the learning environment. Vosko urges
adult educators to respect the "quiet" learner, and Mahoney recommends the
use of positive reinforcement when needed for certain learners.

*Being Proactive in Bringing About Change.* Distorted, inaccurate, or traditional perceptions may exist in the learning environment that lead to
such problems as racism, oppression, exploitation, powerlessness, and learning disadvantages for certain people. Colin and Preciphs urge a commitment to the task of confronting racism by acknowledging that it exists, by
sharing information about all cultures and associated histories, and by
fostering new policies or approaches for administration, teaching, and
evaluation. Collard and Stalker urge adult educators to foster a dialogue on
women's issues, to establish gender-neutral learning environments, and to
examine their daily behavior to see if they disempower or devalue women

learners in any way. These recommendations also have implications for the way language, logic, and curricular materials are used, as well as for the way practitioners, teachers, and professors are trained.

*Making a Personal Commitment to Change.* Several authors discuss the need for adult educators to make personal commitments to changing their views on learning environments and how to work within them. This need may be the most difficult to satisfy because our "practice" approaches, beliefs, and materials typically are well ingrained. However, whether the task is giving up some control to learners, incorporating new technology, confronting personal racist or sexist views, or redoing old curricular materials that may be offensive to certain learners, the commitment to such change should improve our effectiveness as professional adult educators.

## Research Needs

Several requirements for additional research also are apparent in the chapters here.

1. Common definitions and terminology related to the learning environment are needed. A related need is to carry out developmental research on the SPATIAL model presented by Fulton, the "temperature" guide created by Mahoney, and the various checklists offered by many authors in this volume.

2. More research is needed on various issues of physical setting with adult learners as study subjects, such as seat size requirements, crowding, and how learners make personal decisions regarding the space they choose or prefer.

3. We need to better understand the ramifications of changes in the learning environment, as any one change may create new problems for or stresses on learners.

4. We need to know much more about how to help adults feel comfortable with microcomputers and other technological devices, especially if the adults have had little prior experience with this technology.

5. Research on aspects of adult teaching and learning should include subjects of both sexes, as well as from various racial and socioeconomic groupings. Research reported in the literature and from which generalizations are made should clearly indicate the subjects studied.

6. More historical research on women and blacks should be conducted so that their contributions to the development of our discipline are better known.

7. The ways that language, logic, and feedback are used in the classroom should be studied with adult learners to determine if there are qualitative differences in learning styles across various groups.

8. We need to know much more about the impact of racism on the development of practitioners' perceptual patterns and how racism impedes the teaching and learning process.

9. We need to know much more about the learning environment beyond what is addressed in this volume, such as the impact of a learner's social class, financial status, and literacy level on learning potential and on a particular teaching approach.

10. Finally, we need a better understanding of how the learning environment can be changed, including the role of learners, related training implications for teachers, and bureaucratic hurdles that must be overcome.

## Conclusion

The learning environment is a complex interrelationship of several dimensions. Some of this complexity has not yet been explored, nor is it even addressed in this volume. However, we can anticipate that many of the practice suggestions and research needs outlined in this chapter will be instrumental in promoting better understanding and increased effectiveness of adult teaching and learning endeavors.

*Roger Hiemstra is professor of adult education and chair of the adult education graduate program at Syracuse University, Syracuse, New York.*

# INDEX

Aagaard, L., 7, 11
Accessibility, for physically challenged, 26
Adorno, T., 84
Adult Classroom Environment Scale (ACES), 7
Adult Education Association of the United States of America, 18
Adult learning, 1-3, 5-12, 91-97; barriers to, 23-24, 41-42, 51-60; and climate, 41-50; and microcomputers, 33-40; and physical environment, 13-22, 23-32; and racism, 61-70; research needs for, 96-97; resources on, 83-91; and women, 71-81
Agger, B., 84
"Alarm Over Workplace Murders," 74, 80
Alba, R. D., 65, 69
Apps, J. W., 42, 43, 49
Architecture/design, and learning environments, 5, 14. See also Physical environment, Space
Ashcraft, N., 27, 31, 84
Audiovisuals, and adult learning, 5
Authoritarianism, of physical environment, 19-20

Backhouse, C., 75, 78, 80
Baldwin, J., 85
Bartky, S. L., 74, 80
Beaudry, J., 16, 21
Becker, F., 16, 21, 25, 31
Becker, J., 5, 10
Bee, J., 16, 21
Belenky, M. F., 6, 10, 77, 80, 84
Belsheim, D. J., 7, 10
Benhabib, S., 76, 80
Berkhofer, R. F., 61, 69
Blair, G. M., 63, 69
Bordo, S., 74, 80
Bork, A., 33, 40
Borthwick, T., 18, 21
Brockett, R. G., 6, 10
Brookfield, S. D., 44, 49
Brooks, G. C., Jr., 62, 70
Brooks, M., 16, 21
Brown, F. A., Jr., 60

Browne, A., 74, 80
Bulkin, E., 84
Burgess, E. W., 66, 69
Burgess, J. H., 27, 32
Burrows, D., 64, 69, 85
Butterwick, S., 77, 80

Castaldi, B., 85
Checklists, for evaluating learning environments, 21, 30, 38-39, 49, 68
Chickering, A. W., 37, 40
Class conduct: first session of, 45-48, 49; and women, 76-77. See also Climate
Classroom: design of, 17. See also Environments, Physical environment, Seating arrangements, Space
Climate, learning, 2, 5, 6, 7, 42-50, 94
Clinchy, N., 6, 10, 77, 80, 84
Cockburn, C., 73, 80
Colin, S.A.J., III, 1-2, 61, 70, 94, 95
Collaboration, and spaces, 26
Collard, S., 3, 8, 10, 71-81, 94, 95-96
College and University Classroom Environment Inventory (CUCEI), 7
Commission on Architecture, 5, 10
Commission on Non-Traditional Study, 51
Community responsibilities, and adult learners, 52, 58-59
Computers. See Microcomputers
Connell, R. W., 73, 80
Conover, D. W., 12
Conti, C. J., 7, 10
Cooney, N. L., 27, 32
Cooperative Extension, 5
Covey, S, R., 9, 10
Cranton, P., 60
Cross, K. P., 51, 60
Culture, and learning environment, 7, 64
Curricula, and women, 75-76

Damon, A., 5, 10
Darkenwald, G. G., 7, 10
David, T., 7, 10, 15, 17, 21
Davison, C., 18, 22, 89
DeJoy, J. K., 2, 29, 33-40, 94, 95
Delaney, L. T., 61, 69

# ORDERING INFORMATION

NEW DIRECTIONS FOR ADULT AND CONTINUING EDUCATION is a series of paperback books that explores issues of common interest to instructors, administrators, counselors, and policy makers in a broad range of adult and continuing education settings—such as colleges and universities, extension programs, businesses, the military, prisons, libraries, and museums. Books in the series are published quarterly in Fall, Winter, Spring, and Summer and are available for purchase by subscription as well as by single copy.

SUBSCRIPTIONS for 1991 cost $45.00 for individuals (a savings of 20 percent over single-copy prices) and $60.00 for institutions, agencies, and libraries. Please do not send institutional checks for personal subscriptions. Standing orders are accepted.

SINGLE COPIES cost $13.95 when payment accompanies order. (California, New Jersey, New York, and Washington, D.C., residents please include appropriate sales tax.) Billed orders will be charged postage and handling.

DISCOUNTS FOR QUANTITY ORDERS are available. Please write to the address below for information.

ALL ORDERS must include either the name of an individual or an official purchase order number. Please submit your order as follows:
   *Subscriptions:* specify series and year subscription is to begin
   *Single copies:* include individual title code (such as CE1)

MAIL ALL ORDERS TO:
   Jossey-Bass Inc., Publishers
   350 Sansome Street
   San Francisco, California 94104

FOR SALES OUTSIDE OF THE UNITED STATES CONTACT:
   Maxwell Macmillan International Publishing Group
   866 Third Avenue
   New York, New York 10022